Bull Riding

Rodeo's Most Dangerous 8 Seconds

Floyd Cowan

Detselig Enterprises Ltd.

Calgary, Alberta, Canada

Bull Riding

Canadian Cataloguing in Publication

Cowan, Floyd
Bull riding

Includes index.
ISBN 1-55059-179-7

1. Bull riding. 2. Rodeo performers. I. Title.
GV1834.45.B84C68 1999 791.8'4 C99-910180-3

Detselig Enterprises Ltd.
210-1220 Kensington Rd. N.W.
Calgary, Alberta T2N 3P5
www.temerondetselig.com
e-mail: temeron@telusplanet.net
telephone: (403) 283-0900
fax: (403) 283-6947

Detselig Enterprises Ltd. appreciates the financial support for our 1999 publishing program, provided by Canadian Heritage and other sources.

Printed in Canada.

ISBN 1-55059-179-7

SAN 115-0324

Cover design by Dean Macdonald

Table of Contents

The Most Dangerous Sport 7

The Wild West 13

Are You Ready? 17

It's Not If, or When, But How Bad 22

The Fans 27

Jay and Clint 30

Williams Lake 33

The Party Begins 37

Cowboy Christmas 42

Don't Make it Look Too Easy 53

There's No Pain Like It 58

A Leader Among Men 66

A Wise Guy 72

The Big Show 77

The Next Lane Frost 81

Tuffanuff 86

The Johansen Brothers 93
Weekend Whisky 96
A Bowl of Cereal 106
The Bitter End 111
The Darker Side 114
Where Does the Money Go? 117
Jack Daines 121
When Tragedy Hits 128
They Can't Be Tamed 133
The Legends 140
Suicide Sirloin 143
Dancing with the One Ton Tornado 148
You've Got to Have Heart 162
Getting In and Getting Out of the Game 171
Smarter Than His Shirt 175
More Bull 177
Glossary 182

When you add it all up the sport of Pro Rodeo, featuring Bull Riding, makes all other sports look like games.

Jack Daines,
former Bull Rider,
Rodeo Promoter

Many Thanks

It is very difficult for an outsider to get inside and understand a close-knit group such as bull riders. If I've done this with any success, it was due to the helpfulness of the cowboys themselves. They allowed me into their world where I was able to talk to them, listen, and observe them at work and play.

I would like to thank every cowboy and cowgirl that gave me time, and answered my endless questions.

Special thanks to Jay Manning and Clint Ostrem for allowing me to travel with them, share their motel room and let me learn first hand what "going down the road" means. I appreciated their good humor and open honesty.

Thanks to Austin Beasely for letting me tag along with him, and for being patient with my probing and endless questions.

Dave Leader contributed a great deal to *Bull Riding*. Not only did he give me a lot of time as we developed the glossary, but he talked to the other cowboys, telling them what I was doing, and making it easier for me to get the stories I was looking for. I had a number of long and interesting conversations with him.

Don Wise is another person who has made a great contribution. Allowing me to reprint an excerpt from his book on the rodeo, *Chute That Horse*, adds color and a fresh perspective which I believe readers will appreciate. He went out of his way to give me advice and introduce me into the ways of the rodeo that turned out to be very valuable as I floated around the periphery of rodeo society, trying to get in deeper.

Thanks to Grace and Stan Martin for putting me up while I was in Calgary and putting up with me.

The Most Dangerous Sport

"Get her hot boys!" the chute boss hollers. An arid wind blows gritty dust across the infield as the sun burns down in the heat of the afternoon.

The hard pointed hooves of the snorting, bellowing bull sledge hammer against the metal chute. The rage of the 1500 pound animal makes it evident that he doesn't want that cowboy on his back. Foam bubbles from his grinding mouth, he defecates and bellows and bangs out a ringing, raging protest.

Getting a good grip on Rodeo's Most Dangerous 8 Seconds.

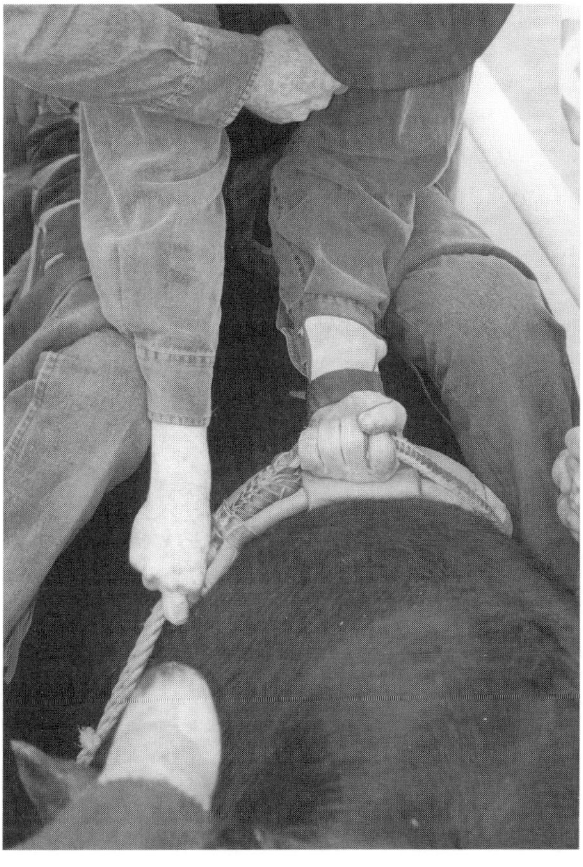

"Bear down! Bear Down!" the men around the chute shout encouragement to the cowboy who is outweighed 10 times by his opponent.

The cowboy's face tightens, he nods his head, the gate flies open and the bull charges into the arena, bucking, spinning, kicking, churning up the earth, doing whatever it can to launch the cowboy. The rider stays on board for eight seconds before using the bull's momentum to dismount and get as far away from him as possible.

On the surface it looks like an uncomplicated sport – all you have to do is get some simple-minded cowboy on a single-minded bull and let the two have a go at it, and the people will come to watch. It is not so simple or easy.

The people do come to watch, resulting in a growth in the popularity of the sport to the extent that now bull riding events are held on their own, without other rodeo competitions.

It is a gruelling sport, hard on the body, hard on the mind and hard on the family. The travelling is unrelenting and unforgiving. Despite all this, despite the injuries, the pain, the time in the hospital, being broke and thousands of miles from home, the cowboys just want to get on that bull again. And again.

What you can't see from the stands are the complexities of a sport that involves three distinct groups of athletes – the bull riders, the bulls and the bullfighters. Behind them is a support group and together they have evolved this event into a sport that is considered the most dangerous in North America, in the opinion of sports writers. It has also been tagged as "The Most Exciting 8 Seconds" and "The Richest 8 Seconds" in pro sports.

The most commonly asked question put to bull riders is *why* they get on an animal that seems intent on killing them. Why do they get on an animal that is so much bigger and stronger than themselves to risk life and limb for very little money?

This is where I began. When I started researching this book I went to the Luxton Fair on Vancouver Island and this was the question I wanted answered. What I learned is that it is only one of many fascinating aspects of the sport. While the riders, ex-riders and the devoted fans know the sport in intimate detail, most Canadians know very little about it at all.

When I mentioned to friends and acquaintances that I was doing a book on bull riders, many people thought I was writing about Spanish bullfighters, a very different sport from the one practised in Canada. In Spain the career of a bull is very short. The rodeo career of bulls can be as much as 10 years.

As in any good sport there are legends and the legendary. Legendary bulls and legendary riders. In Canada, names from the past such as Girletz, Garstad, Johansen and Snyder are the fence posts to the rising stars of today who are making their own stories on bulls that are becoming tougher, meaner and smarter. There are American legends, such as the great Lane Frost, who every young rider wants to emulate, the even better Tuff Hedeman, and eight-time world champion Don Gay.

If the bulls had their own hall of fame, names such as Gerdy, Hagar and Tiger would be there, along with the rankest of them all, Bodacious – the only bull to be retired because he was just too mean. And there would be a place for the almost unridable Red Rock. Rambo, Sugar Ray Skoal and Dodge Ram Tough have earned their places.

Stock contractors not only breed and raise the bulls but take pride in them the same as they would any protégé. As much as they like to see a cowboy give a good ride, they also like to see their bull give the cowboy an outstanding trip. Canadian stock contractors have made their names on both sides of the border and the Vold name is respected in Canada and the U.S., where two generations of the family have raised outstanding stock. Girletz, Northcott, Franklin and Big Stone Rodeo are names that have been long familiar to rodeogoers.

The bullfighters are the unsung heros of the sport. Their contribution sometimes even goes unnoticed by the cowboys whose lives they are saving. And they do save lives. Watching them run around the arena, there may seem to be no method to their madness, but it is not a haphazard flurry of activity by the men in rags, but the use of specific techniques to keep the cowboy out of harm's way.

Despite their efforts cowboys do get gored by the bulls, which was the cruel and sudden end of Lane Frost. Being killed is a rare occurrence in the

The bullfighters do their job at the Williams Lake Stampede.

sport, and with the advent of flack jackets and well-trained bullfighters, serious injuries have been reduced. However, simply getting on a bull begins a journey that gives the body a serious pounding, it strains muscles and ligaments, breaks bones and hearts, and often rattles the brain and embroils the emotions.

The most dangerous sport has another casualty. The top ranked professional cowboys in Canada have to get to 100 or so rodeos a year in order to win enough money to support themselves and to win sufficient points to qualify for the Canadian Finals Rodeo or to the World Championships. In a typical weekend the cowboy may attend three rodeos several hundred miles apart. On a long weekend they may get to four or five events covering thousands of miles. Going down the road is part of the lifestyle, and while I worked on this book, it became part of mine, though not to the extent that it is for the bull riders. Travelling is part of the story, a very important part, and there are lots of stories about being on the road, and I have gathered but a few. If you want to hear more, get to know a cowboy, but be prepared to wait for awhile because often the cowboy isn't a talker and it is only late at night or on a long stretch between yesterday's ride and tomorrow's that the stories begin to come out.

The constant travelling is hard on the family life, and when a cowboy gets married they often have to make a choice, the rodeo or their marriage. This is one of the reasons the young cowboys don't like to commit themselves to any one young lady.

When I began this book I knew less than nothing about the sport of bull riding. I had misconceptions and little knowledge and no experience of the world they live in. Not only did I learn a great deal about the sport, but I learned a few new things about Canada and the complex society we enjoy.

Travelling between Victoria and Williams Lake and then Victoria and Calgary was like being dipped in cold water, taken out again and dipped once more. You notice the difference. The cowboys and their lifestyle is distinctly different from "urban" Canada. I even hate to say "urban" because there are "urban" cowboys. There are cowboys who live in the city but ride in the rodeo, and during the off season many cowboys work in the city as there is not enough work on the ranch to keep them gainfully employed. Many ranchers have other trades or occupations.

It is not so easy to label bull riders, but there are common attitudes and attributes which distinguish the rodeo contestants from mainstream Canada. Most of the bull riders I met, with a few exceptions, were young men. They displayed a greater maturity and self confidence than most young Canadians. They very seldom complained about anything, whereas it seems most Canadians complain about everything. Not that I asked, but politics never once became part of the conversation, and I had some long and wide-ranging conversations with a number of people. The rodeo world is a distinct culture from the rest of Canada, and I believe there are lessons that can be learned from it.

One of the contrasts that I found very striking was to go from talking with young men who didn't have a dollar to their name but would find a way to get to the next rodeo in the hope that they might win enough money to keep them going to the next, then I would be on Douglas Street in the heart of Victoria and stepping around young people camped on the sidewalk begging for spare change.

The attitude I liked the most was demonstrated after a bull rider had a particularly tough time. They would limp out of the arena and say, "well if it was easy, everyone would do it." They were not deterred because it was difficult, but they were invigorated by the challenge. There is a large segment of Canadian society that prefers the safety and security of achieving mediocrity, or nothing at all, and seeks to do nothing that has any challenge whatsoever.

The working title of this book was *Bull*, and while the cowboys, and especially their wives and girlfriends, liked the double meaning I found little that was disingenuous about the bull riders. They were very straightforward. I had no reason to doubt the truth of what they told me as it meshed completely with what I observed. If I was given any bull, it was not from the men who climbed on the backs of these powerful animals, but from the people around them.

What follows is the story about bull riding, the places I went, the people I met, the stories they told me. There is a growing interest in bull riding and thousands of people watch it every year. So, let's Go Down the Road and travel into the unique and fascinating world of the bull rider.

The Wild West

I didn't have to go too far to get to Luxton Rodeo, the only Pro Rodeo event on Vancouver Island, but distances are not always measured in miles. The quiet and pretty tree-lined streets of Victoria, with their outdoor cafes and hanging flower baskets, are light years distant in attitude to the open spaces, the dust and the noise of the Luxton Fair Grounds on the edge of the city's suburbs.

Three days before the rodeo began I phoned Sandy West, co-manager with Charlie Price of the Luxton Rodeo Committee, and explained that I was writing a book about the bull riders and wanted to know if I could get a press pass to the rodeo.

Sandy was not impressed in the least. "Every year I get a lot of requests for passes, and then I never see any stories or pictures. People just want to get in free, it costs $10.00 to get in." There was a hard edge to her voice that was difficult to ignore.

I talked some more, explaining the book I wanted to do. She didn't seem any more impressed and certainly the edge to her voice had softened none, but she told me to come out to her office at 1:00 p.m.

On the fair grounds the large trucks of the carnival had arrived and there was a slow energy as they still had lots of time to get ready before they opened for business.

The door to the trailer I had been directed to was open. Two men in blue jeans and striped shirts sat at chairs in front of a desk. They both had cans of Coors Light in hand. Behind the desk sat a wiry middle-aged blonde lady with a tanned western look about her. I had never met Sandy West, but I had no doubt that this was her. She could not have had a more descriptive name for her appearance or her position.

"Hi . . ." was as far as I got before she cut me off.

"You'rc thc guy I talkcd to this morning?"

"Yes."

She got up and went to a file cabinet behind her and came back with a sheet of paper and a small card. She asked me my name, wrote it down on the card and the sheet and handed it to me.

"Do you want to see some of my writing?" I wanted to assure her I was serious about this and not just out to get a free pass. Though if I had to spend $10 every day just to write my story it wasn't going to be a very profitable enterprise.

"Not right now."

One of the two Coors drinkers snickered.

"I'm having a meeting."

I took my pass and beat it back to my rental car, where I took the time to look at it. It was a complementary ONE DAY pass.

"Damn," I muttered. I wanted to learn about the heart and soul of the bull riders. You don't get to know people in an afternoon. "Well, I guess I'll go to the first day, try to make contact and see what happens from there." I drove back into the city, dreaming up ways I could get in for free the other days.

If I wasn't enamored with Sandy West, there were a lot of people who were. In 1996 Sandy was chosen Committee Person of the Year, and for good reason. Rodeo has a long history on Vancouver Island, and specifically at Luxton. In 1993 Sandy and the Rodeo Committee committed themselves to turning their rodeo professional. Sandy has dedicated herself to making Luxton a profitable rodeo, doing everything she can to make it work. She has organized dances and cleaned the halls afterwards.

All the people who work on the Committee under Sandy and Charlie are volunteers and there wouldn't be a rodeo without them. They take tickets at the gates, they work in the arena and beer gardens, there are electricians and carpenters and many more volunteering their time just to make sure the rodeo happens.

The cost and the inconvenience of B.C. Ferries makes it difficult and expensive for competitors and stock contractors to get to Vancouver Island. And, on the same weekend, the Victoria Day long weekend, there are two rodeos on the mainland. A hospitality tent welcomes the competitors and they are given a feast of seafood, chili, hot potatoes, vegetables, beef, pork and chicken – so they get something for making that extra effort to get to Vancouver Island, even if they don't make it into the prize money.

Sandy has been helping to organize the Luxton Rodeo for over 20 years and was responsible for the rodeo continuing when it was in danger of being canceled. She says she was not prepared to see rodeo disappear from the

Island, and through determination and a survival instinct that would not let her give up, she managed to convince others to continue.

I mused over the possibilities. Perhaps one of the local papers would be interested in a feature story. I ruled out the *Goldstream Gazette* as this was their territory and they were sure to have already assigned someone.

I wondered if John Arnett was still at the *Sooke Mirror*. I got a recent copy and saw that John's name was not listed in any capacity. The following morning I phoned. Rod, the publisher, wasn't in. And it was editor Mitch Moneo's day off.

"Would you like to leave a message?" the receptionist asked.

I explained what I was doing and said I would phone back later.

About an hour later I went through the entire story again, this time with Rod listening. "I think it's better if you talk to my editor, Mitch Moneo. It's his day off today, but if you give him a call tomorrow I will have had a chance to talk to him and we'll see what we can do for you."

When I phoned the following morning, now Friday and getting close to Day One of the rodeo, I asked Mitch if Rod had talked to him about me.

"No, he hasn't."

My spiel was getting quite slick by this point. I launched into the story once again.

"I'll tell you what to do," Mitch cut me short when he caught on. "Give Keith Norbury at the *Goldstream Gazette* a call . . ."

"I would've thought he'd have his own reporter going."

"He called me asking if I had anyone who could cover it for him."

It took a couple of calls to get through to Keith, and the excitement I felt at the thought that I might get press credentials were stomped on like a rodeo dummy's head by a rampaging bull.

"I've got someone covering it," Keith told me. "As a matter of fact they are over at the Westwind at a press conference which starts in about 10 minutes."

Oh well, I thought, back to Plan A.

"But they're both photographers," he continued. "I wouldn't need a news report. Because of our deadlines, it wouldn't get in until the following week."

"Yeah, I'd be happy to give you a feature story in exchange for a press pass."

"I'll see what I can do," he promised. "I'll give you a call this afternoon."

I was out the rest of the day and when I came back that evening there was no message on the answering machine.

Another return trip to Plan A. I was going to have to make a lot of shuttles between Plan A, Plan B and Plan C as I travelled between Place A, Place B and Place C. But frequent changes of plans were not going to deter me from getting the story. I was determined to do this book and wouldn't be put off by people who kept getting in my way.

Are You Ready?

Saturday morning, first day of the Rodeo, and I'm without wheels. I take a two hour trip on city buses to get to the grounds. It gives me time to think about what I'm doing. I worry about working on a project with no guarantee of getting a pay day when the job is done and I've got to pay for everything on the way. There is no fat expense account to ease the hardship of travel. I didn't realize it then, but this is what the cowboys feel as they go down the road entering rodeos with no guarantee of making money and having to pay their own way. They do it day after day, year after year, throughout their career.

Long before you get to the fair, it comes to you. The noise in the distance clarifies itself into the tinny music of the rides, the calling of the barkers enticing people to play – and pay, the squeals and laughter of children – and adults – caught up in the excitement, the crackle of electricity, and the clanging, banging, popping, whooping, shooting, clatter and rattle of games. There is an anticipation of excitement, an anticipation which usually exceeds the delivery.

To my surprise there are no animal rights protesters at the grounds, as there have been at other rodeos in other years. It appears they may have given up the fight.

I go to the trailer that serves as the Rodeo Committee's office to see if the *Gazette* has arranged a press pass for me and arrive at the same time as two journalists. I have my camera slung around my neck and undoubtedly look very professional in my blue jeans and t-shirt. A friendly lady greets us and tells a volunteer to take "the press" through the gate. I trail along with them chatting with a local radio reporter. We are all stamped on the hand and admitted to the grounds where the day's events are about to get underway. I didn't have to use my pass, so I knew I'd be back the following day.

I begin by annoying as many people as I can at one time by walking back and forth around the arena, everywhere spectators are allowed and trying to figure out how I could get into areas where we weren't allowed.

There is no way. It just isn't possible. Everything is tightly controlled, the result of four lawsuits, I'm told, against the Luxton by people who have been injured by animals. One kid was bit seriously enough to inspire a lawsuit.

Most of the seating runs down the east side of the infield. This is where the families sit. All the seats in the grandstand, in the shade, are taken. On the west side the drinking of beer is allowed, so children aren't. This is where I spend most of my time.

The beer-drinking fans look a little rougher than the folks with the baby carriages and they look a little happier – sometimes a lot happier. The hair is a little longer, a little less well kept, and if you don't have a beer in hand you are looked upon as being somewhat suspect. When the rodeo clown, T Texas Terry, wants audience participation, it is to this side of the arena that he comes, and gets the liveliest volunteers. One volunteer loses her panties to the clown. Or were they his panties?

The attitudes are distinctly different on either side of the arena. When a little calf, beating it hell for leather, is suddenly, roughly and dramatically jerked off its feet by the lasso around its neck and lands heavily in the dust, a sorrowful and sympathetic "oooohhhh" drifts across from the east stands to the west.

"Don't say that!" snaps a tough looking lady sitting behind me. "I can't stand that!" she growls. She doesn't have to explain her sentiments to the people sitting around her. They nod in agreement, and there is some mumbling about bleeding hearts. "If they don't like it, they shouldn't come to the rodeo!"

The announcer creates a lot of the excitement at the rodeo. I realize how important his contribution is when the sound system malfunctions for ten minutes and a vast emptiness invades all the space his voice had filled. Without him there is no focus, it is like a ballet without music.

"Look how strong that cowboy is," Bill Kehler draws the attention of everyone to the chute where a bucking horse is kicking and fussing before the cowboy has settled into the saddle. "He just picked up that horse with one hand. That's one tough cowboy."

There is a place for photographers, a wooden box, raised a few feet higher than the fence, but it is crowded, not with people taking pictures, so I sit in the stands where there are photographers standing on the top row of the white wooden planks, while others are kneeling on the grass, poking their lenses through the wire fence, ignoring the signs telling people not to stand or sit along the fence. Everyone else dutifully obeys.

The blue sky is without a wrinkle, making it a perfect day for photography and for the rodeo.

"When that cowboy comes out the gate his horse is going about 35 miles an hour," Kehler tells the crowd. The steer wrestler then leans way over the steer who is beating it for the other end of the infield as fast as his hooves can take him, the cowboy leans over then leaps on its back, grabbing him by the horns, or the head, or wherever he can get a good hold of, and twists the steer into the dust.

Doesn't work perfectly all the time. Occasionally the steer wins the race and has a laugh as he trots off through the gate at the opposite end of the arena. Sometimes the steer just refuses to go down and stands there, head twisted to one side while a frustrated cowboy expends a lot of energy on an animal that isn't going anywhere.

Even when the cowboy does his work well, it is not without its danger. The steer's horns may be blunted, but they are harder than most human hides. One big cowboy gets up out of the dust, after flipping the steer to the ground, a ragged rip running horizontally through the vertical blue stripes of his shirt. A tear like that probably did his skin no good either.

There is a ritual in the arena, or so it seems to me, after watching the first few events. It doesn't matter how a contestant did, if they had a record-breaking time or missed completely, they'd get up slowly, slower if injured, dust themselves off, and that dusting goes longer the more hurt they are or the worse the performance, then they slowly, sometimes limping, slouched slightly forward, trudge over and pick up their cowboy hat, shake off the dust, gather any other equipment that may be laying around, and make their way to the fence. They have the luxury of time that the bull riders don't.

If they've done well the announcer might give them a bit of encouragement and they take off their hat and raise it high in the air in acknowledgment and the crowd responds with warm applause.

If they've had a particularly bad performance the announcer gives the contestant encouragement, the crowd applauds and they lumber through the soft dirt with a bit of something for their efforts. But not much.

The cowboys sit on the rails in rows like crows on a telephone line, speaking not much more than the cowboy getting ready for the calf roping event – the tie rope held tightly between the teeth.

Even the 14-16-year-old boys, who ride the steers, know that you don't leave the arena whimpering. One lad gets stepped on pretty solid, his face contorts in pain as he limps off – most of the effort is to keep back the tears. But he's back the next day, this time sticking for the eight seconds.

Steer riding at the Luxton Pro Rodeo, on Vancouver Island.

The volunteers hustle about – kicking photographers out of places they shouldn't be and keeping fans and reporters from areas they'd like to get into. The volunteers are not quite insiders, they get closer to the action than the general public, but there is a distinct gap between them and the cowboys.

The audience at Luxton is different from those in the Interior and out on the Prairies. Some people come out from the city for the day, just for an outing. Waiting in line for the washroom, I ask the middle-aged fellow ahead of me what he likes best about the rodeo.

"Nothing," he growls over his shoulder. "My wife likes it."

Others are real rodeo fans. They may have been involved with it at one time, some of them study it, follow the big names, know the animals and think they could score a ride as good as any professional judge. They are dedicated fans, out for more than a good time, they come every day and don't miss a minute. Though some people may have someone particular they are cheering for, most people are there just to see a good performance. Everyone cheers for the cowboy. They want to see him win, but they do appreciate a good show by the animals.

"Are you ready for the bull riding?" Bill Kehler demands of the crowd.

The crowd shouts and hollers. They're ready!

"Are you ***really*** ready for the Bull Riding?" Bill gets the audience worked up. The music pounds, the bullfighters and T Texas Terry get in place. The real action is about to begin!

This is what they've come for. They've come to see 1500 pounds of flesh explode into the arena with a 150 lb cowboy hanging desperately onto it, fighting with all his strength to go the distance. They're here to see a mean bull take a run at the bullfighters, trying to give them a good hooking. They're with Rob Mitchell for the length of the ride as he goes for 8 seconds. If they've been following bull riding for any length of time, they know Quentin Lowry of High River, Alberta, and Austin Beasley, not only one of Canada's best bull riders, but one who is making a mark in the U.S.

"Ooh," sympathetically rises from the stands when a cowboy hits the dust. They ride with the cowboys, moving about in their seats as the rider is jolted about on the bull.

Kehler is keeping the audience informed on the rider's scores and giving bits of info on their background as they prepare for their ride.

A break is taken in the middle of the rides and a pick-up truck is driven into the arena. It is time for the 50/50 draw, another little event unique to this part of the world. A rather large lady sits in the back of the pick-up.

A mouthy man in the drinking section calls out, "Is that to show us the payload?"

The fans are restless, especially those who spent a lot of money on the 50/50 tickets and didn't win anything. They want the bull riding to continue, and it doesn't take long before Manhattan is tossing a cowboy into the dirt. Dave Leader is having a tough time getting settled on his mount and he's off before they get a few steps out of the chute. Bernie Bowe doesn't make the eight seconds and his money is dwindling away, being out of the running once again. Locklin MacIntosh scores a 78 and isn't the only one to go away happy. The fans have loved it. They are pumped. This was great! Tomorrow many of them will be back again, just to see the bull riding.

The bull riding is always the last event at the rodeo and when the last bull has trotted back into the pens the crowd quickly disperses. Some go off to the fair, most go home.

It is time for me to really get to work, which means going to the beer garden.

You're a fool if you think you're not going to be hurt

Rick Henderson
Bull Rider

It's Not If, or When, But How Bad

BJ Smith walks like he's a bag of sticks and bricks. Kind of bent forward, moving stiffly, as if he's made of wire that's all rusted up. That's what 15 years of riding the bulls will do for you, especially if you've had some close encounters of the worst kind. "It isn't when you're going to get hurt," BJ states, "It's how bad you're going to get hurt."

I sit in the beer garden, a tent with a dirt floor that smells more of beer than of garden, with picnic tables with plastic coverings. Across the table are two guys who seemed a bit bored with the whole scene. We nod at each other and a conversation ensues. When I tell them what I am doing, Gregg Mah says, "Do you want to meet a cowboy?"

"Yeah, sure."

"Hey BJ," he calls to a cowboy across the room. "There's a guy from the press. He'd like to talk to you."

BJ ambles over and sits down at the next picnic table. He isn't sure he wants to talk to me. There is a shy, quiet quality to his eyes. They are a mask to his inner world, not a window to his soul.

"What do you wanna know?" He smiles, kind of shy and uneasy.

"How long you been riding?"

"About 15 years. I started on the sheep, then I did the steers, then the bulls. Yeah, I was a Mutton Buster," it is a rueful admission, tinged with a touch of pride.

"Did you see that kid out there today?" We all talk at once about the four-year-olds. They are put on the backs of sheep, wearing helmets a size

Bull riders often start their career as a mutton buster. Luxton Pro Rodeo.

too large. Most kids go about two and a half steps and one, maybe two bleats from the sheep, who seems to want to have none of this at all, before falling off. Today, one kid had two fistfuls of raw wool and he hung on while the sheep shot down the arena like a cat with its tail on fire. When the horn sounded, sheep and kid were still going at full speed. It delighted the crowd, the kid looked bemused at the whole affair and the sheep didn't wait around to give its opinion.

"My parents have got a ranch up in Courtenay," BJ continues. "I've been doing this since I was a kid, but I had some good teachers, Larry Mahan and Donny Gay, and Sonny before he died."

The brim of his tan cowboy hat bends down as if it is meant to have the rain run off. The more he talks, the more he relaxes and I keep asking him questions until he realizes he does have something to say, and if there is a silence he can count on me to ask a question so he doesn't get uncomfortable in a prolonged silence, which he might be expected to fill.

"Oh, I've had a lot of broken bones. It'd be a lot easier to count the ones that aren't broken. I'm still walking and I'm still moving. I'm 42 years old now. I'm going to hate to see what I'll be like when old age hits.

"I got busted up two years ago and I don't move quite as good as I used to. I'm not riding right now cause it didn't heal up quite the way I thought it should. I work the chutes and I do a lot of work in the arena, helping the riders, taking care of the animals."

"What was your first ride like? What were you thinking?"

"Come on, be truthful," Gregg interjects in a teasing tone.

The guarded look returns to BJ's eyes. Are we going to make fun of him?

"I was getting my rigging set up and I looked over at my buddy who was pulling up the rope and I thought, 'what the fuck am I doing here?' They said, 'Cowboy head down.' I nodded my hat, and I went. Everything went so fast after that I didn't have time to think."

I drink some beer and leave a moment of dead air and BJ suddenly becomes more animated, but he's still talking in a soft undertone. "The one thing people don't understand is how goddamned dangerous this sport is. We're in the same category as Gretzky, but we don't get the recognition and we don't get the big paydays unless we win.

"We train, just like you would in any sport. I run with leg weights and I use a tennis ball – that's to strengthen your grip hand. And I work on the farm throwing bails. I keep in shape that way."

I want to know how important winning is. Has he ridden hurt?

"Oh yeah. You get busted up and you go back in there, you're trying to make a payday," he looks at Gregg. "There was that guy, the bull came over on his leg and broke it. We wrapped it back up and he went in and rode again. We live with elastic bandages. There isn't a guy that isn't walking around with a whole kit of them."

BJ Smith learned to ride the bulls from some of the sport's great riders.

The average bull rider risks life and limb for $15-20 000 a year, according to BJ. The top cowboys can make a lot more. Winning the Shoot Out at Calgary brings a $50 000 payday, but only the best riders get invited to that show.

"I'd do 50 to 150 rodeos a year. We pay to play the game, unlike the hockey players, who get the big pay cheques. I got no use for those pricks. I'd like them to go a round with us, see how long they last."

He takes out a package of chewing tobacco and puts a thick wad into the corner of his mouth. Offers some to Gregg, who declines. Doesn't bother offering me any.

"Heaven's Door nailed me about two years ago," the cowboy looks at the world with a thoughtful wariness. "Broke my hip, blew out my knee and broke three ribs. He put me right through the goal posts. Talk about a field goal!" He spits out a long stream on the dirt floor of the beer garden.

"How long did you spend in the hospital?"

"Didn't go to the hospital. I did later to have my hip put back in place, but then I didn't go. I got up, shook it off, but I was in a world of hurt the next morning."

"How long was it before you rode again?"

"Oh, I rode two more times that day. It was the adrenaline. I didn't start hurting until later, and suddenly my leg wouldn't work, and I said, 'whoooa, something's not right here.'"

But why does he get on an animal that seems intent on killing him?

"It's the jazz and the working with the animals," he chews thoughtfully, those wary eyes look at his friends who are listening with interest. "Some people think that I want to be the centre of attention, but hey, when I'm out there I never hear or see the crowd. It's a personal thing between me and the animal. He outweighs you by a ton, but if you can keep your head together, and you've done your training and you put all these things together and beat him – that's the jazz."

I ask him about the protesters who have shown up at rodeos, upset over the treatment the animals get at the rodeo. These are not people BJ cares for. "Hey, we take real good care of those animals. They're our bread and butter and we're not going to do anything to hurt them. We had the Red Cross around here inspecting them and they gave us an A+ rating. You don't hear that in any of the media," he says it all quite calmly; there is no agitation or emotion in his voice. Then he adds in an undertone, "I ain't got no use for tree huggers."

A misconception BJ would like to clear up is that bulls are dumb. "They are not as stupid as a lot of people think they are. They'll watch you, and if they sense any fear in you they are going to play on it. The day I got nailed I walked out to have a look at the bulls. I didn't know it at the time but Heaven's Door, the one that put me through the goal posts, he followed me all around the field. I rode him last year and I beat him. If they beat me, I'll come back again and beat the bastards."

"What do you like in a bull?"

"I work closely to the line. I'm trying to react to where the bull is going to go, to the right or the left. Is he going to hold back, then explode? The way I see it, a bull is like a good woman, they always keep you guessing. They got their own language. He can still put you down when you're walking."

"What about the other riders? What'd ya think of them?"

He spits, "Hey, we're competing out there for a living, but they'll turn around and help everyone out in the chute. They'll help anyone out in any way. Rigging, they'll borrow it off you. Sometimes guys'll even borrow your horse. That's the way they are. Good people. Good solid people."

Gregg asks, "If you had a son would you want him to ride the bulls?"

BJ thinks about this. "If he wanted to. You'd have to bring him up properly and train him into it."

"Would you ride?" I ask Gregg.

"No, no way."

BJ excuses himself, "I'll be around for the next two days. You need anything, you just ask."

"I like the rodeo," Gregg says. "If you're going to do a book on rodeos you got to go to the Cheesaw Rodeo, it's just across the border, out in the wilds. There are no hotels or places to stay, you have to take your own tent. It's a week long and it's got the greatest atmosphere, they've got live music. Fiddlers and country bands. It's the greatest time. I haven't been there for a couple of years. It's held sometime in July."

The Fans

It's intermission at Day Two of the Luxton Rodeo. The weather has held out again, sunny and dry and the families and the fans are out in numbers to enjoy the events. In the middle of the arena T Texas Terry is blowing up watermelons.

I drift into the beer gardens, pulled by the thought of a cold beer. I find a place to sit and take in the scene.

I've been away from Canada for a long time, and it strikes me how Canadian this all is, the dirt floor, the picnic benches, the beer gardens; where else in the world would the drinkers be segregated, penned in a rather dubious "garden." There is lots of Canadian and Coors. Coors? One of rodeo's sponsors. You see them everywhere. There's the Coors "Man in the Can," the can being the barrel the clowns climb into when the bulls want to rough something up. It is designed like a Coors beer can. Great sponsors, lousy beer.

Lots of people standing around jawing with each other. You might see similar scenes in the United States, but not likely anywhere else in the world. And if the scene isn't distinct enough, the people certainly are. Nowhere are there people like Canadians, and going to the rodeo brings that strongly home to me. Everyone talks with everyone else, whether they've known each other all their lives or if they just happen to be sharing a table. And they've all got an opinion.

Three people sit down at my table, two women and a man, and when they get comfortable, and into their beer, I ask them what they like about the rodeo.

"I love the rodeo," Birdie laughs, "It's the cowboys and their tight little butts. That's what I like."

"Yes," agrees Pattie. "It's the cowboys in their tight Wrangler jeans."

Aaron, not surprisingly, doesn't agree with the ladies.

When I thought I wasn't going to get much serious out of them Pattie says, "My favorite event is the bull riding. It's man over beast. They should have more bull riders and they should tell us more about how they are riding rather than who's winning."

Pattie gets into the conversation. She leans forward over the table, "I've seen too many men hurt by the bulls, you don't like to see that. But you do want to see a rider get a good mark, and if he does get in trouble you like to see him use his head and get out of it."

But it is the possibility of a cowboy getting hurt that adds to the excitement.

Pattie is the first to tell me about Lane Frost and the movie *Eight Seconds*. "It's a great movie," is her opinion. "It's a true story. It shows all the trials and tribulations of being a bull rider. Lane was the best bull rider ever. He rode Red Rock, who had never been ridden for the eight seconds. Lane did it."

I accept her view because I don't know any better. I was to later change my mind.

"Have you been to many bull rides?" I ask.

"Oh yeah. We go whenever we can and we watch it on TV."

"One time we were in Vegas. The bull went down on top of the rider. When the bull came up the rider was still on him and he rode for the eight seconds. His mark was 69. You should've heard the crowd!" She says with intensity. "One of the things I like about bull riding is that it is not a team competition. It gives the individual the opportunity to shine. If the cowboys accrue all their points they can make some serious money."

Birdie says the sport is big and getting bigger. "We watch it a lot on TV. There are bull rides from Mesquite to Texas and everything in between."

I finish my beer and go back out in the sun, walking down the stands in front of the shirt sleeve crowd. They're not dressed as 'western' as the crowds I'll see at other rodeos, but there are a few cowboy hats in the crowd and a lot of blue jeans.

I go up into the wooden booth that is the preserve of photographers and there are a couple of volunteers hanging over the sill looking out at the arena.

The warm spring afternoon drifts along through the other events until the bull riding is to begin and everyone sits up and pays attention. People stride out of the beer gardens, they return from the fair grounds, they don't go to the washroom. They focus their attention on the end of the arena where the bulls are kicking up a fuss.

I want to know what is happening down there, behind the chutes. What are the cowboys going through? What are they thinking? What are they doing to get prepared? I curse my luck for being stuck up here in the stands. I'm agitated.

The fans are right where they want to be; sitting in the sunshine, enjoying an afternoon of bull riding.

Doug McKie from Kinsella, Alberta, comes out on ATM. He's bucked and as he picks himself out of the dust and scampers for safety, ATM is close on his heels. The crowd roars.

"He came awfully close to getting an ivory enema there," Bill Kehler quips when Doug has made it safely to the fence.

They love it.

Marty Ward has a prickly ride on Cactus and Kelly McEwen gives his usual solid performance.

Back in the beer gardens, I talk to Andy Belfie and to Darwin, whose last name I didn't get. Darwin, now a fireman, rode the bulls for awhile and he attended the Johansen's School of Bull Riding. This is the first time I hear the Johansen name, but it was not to be the last. The five Johansen brothers were to be mentioned time and again by bull riders, and always referred to with the greatest respect.

A couple of kids are annoying the calves in the pen while their parents stand by and watch. BJ Smith walks by and tells them to leave the calves alone. He sees me and he says, "People think they're goddamned house pets." Then he changes his tone and asks me how it's going.

"Fine."

"If there is anything I can do for you, you let me know," he slaps me on the shoulder and walks away.

Two Koreans have come to see the rodeo. "What did you think?" I ask.

"I love the rodeo," one laughs. "I love the bull riding." He raises one hand over his head and waves it in the air. "I want to ride a bull."

I don't think he ever has to worry about that actually happening.

Jay and Clint

On the final day of the bull riding I walk close to the fence near the gates where the cowboys go when they finish. I ask around to see if they can arrange to have some of the bull riders talk to me.

"I don't know if they are going to want to stay around for very long," one of the volunteers says. "They like to get away as fast as they can as they've got to get to the next rodeo. But I'll see what I can do."

Today the bulls are in a mood for strutting their stuff. Bill Kehler keeps the crowd warmed up. I'm kneeling by the fence close to the chutes when one of the bulls, who has bucked his rider, looks about, looking for something to take a run at. He sees me. I want to take his picture, but I decide it is best not to move. For a moment I feel a personal relationship with him. I get the sense of the bull's power and attitude. His attitude is, "if you want a fight, so do I, so let's go."

I don't want to fight. But being face to face with the bull, with a fence between you, cannot be half as thrilling as being *enclosed* in that space with him. It makes it understandable why the cowboys scramble for the fence, sometimes on all fours, with such energy when they don't know where the bull is or what he is doing.

Code Red decides that having tossed his rider, he isn't going back into the pen. He trots around the arena glaring at everyone along the fence. He is strong. His muscles ripple like a well-conditioned athlete's.

"I've got a mother-in-law bigger than that," Kehler quips. I don't know if that explains why Bill spends so much time travelling.

When Code Red won't leave centre stage, the pick-up men come in and lasso him, the rope coming right across his eyes, which annoys the hell of him. He falls. The rope is tightened. He bellows and refuses to get to his feet. The tightening noose irritates him so he reluctantly gets to his feet. But he isn't going quietly into that dark pen. With the cowboy on horseback pulling him towards the pen, Code Red runs forward, does a tremendous leap in the air, then lands in a cloud of dust on his side. The crowd responds with laughter and clapping. Code Red has his moment. He lumbers to his feet and trots placidly back to the quiet of the pens without further fanfare.

When the riding is over I am getting ready to pack up and go home, thinking that none of the cowboys will talk to me, but to my surprise a guy at the gate waves to me, "I've got a couple of bull riders that will talk to you."

"Hello," they both say and I begin to notice the things that distinguish bull riders from other people. They stand differently, they walk differently – not just those that are all busted up, but all of them. There is an attitude here, but it is not an aggressive, threatening, in-your-face attitude. It is more one of quiet confidence.

I was surprised at how young they seemed. They were fresh faced and not the image that I had of the gnarled, weather-beaten cowboy. They didn't walk like BJ Smith, they sauntered.

"What's your name?" I ask one.

"Jay Manning."

"How old are you?"

"26."

"How long you been riding?"

"13 years. I started out on the steers."

"How often do you ride in a season."

"Between 50 to 100 times."

"What makes a good bull rider?"

"A big heart."

I had no idea I was talking to the Canadian Champion. There was nothing in the bearing, attitude or face of the smiling young man from Edson, Alberta, to suggest that he was one of the top riders in the country. There was no swagger. He never brought it up, perhaps he thought I knew. But I was still trying to figure out if this was a story worth doing and I had a lot to learn. A hell of a lot.

The interview with Clint Ostrem covers much the same ground.

"Why do you ride bulls?" I asked.

"Somebody's got to do it, I guess," he responds. "It's a good sport. A bit of a thrill."

"What makes a good bull rider?"

"Focus and determination."

"Do you remember your first ride?"

"Not so much my first ride, but the first time I rode the bulls I won the damn thing, and I got hooked."

Bull riders Clint Ostrem (left) and Jay Manning, enjoying their great adventure at the Luxton Pro Rodeo.

I'm impressed with their good nature, their openness and the feeling that they are in the middle of a great adventure and they are enjoying every minute of it. They pause long enough to have their picture taken but then they rush off to the next rodeo to enjoy the thrill of spending eight seconds on the back of a bull.

I walk away feeling dissatisfied. I couldn't learn what I needed by spending two minutes with them. The longer I am able to spend doing an interview the better the story is. What I need to do is get in behind the chutes, to travel with them, go drinking with them, see them in their private moments when they are talking with each other, and not to me.

My dissatisfaction deepened over the next couple of weeks. I was beginning to think that this was a project that was going nowhere. I knew the stories were there. The people and the lifestyle are different from those of mainstream Canada. I wanted to know more.

In my conversations with publishers I finally got some expressions of interest. Encouraged, I packed my bags and headed for Williams Lake. Williams Lake was to be everything that Luxton wasn't and I would begin to do the things that I had to do in order to get to the heart of this sport.

Keen eyed, careless, self-reliant, tuned to vast solitudes, calmly facing dangers and enduring hardships alone and unsung, lording it over horse and brute on the fringe of the world, taking life in one hand while rolling a cigarette in the other, sweating on round ups and freezing on feeding-grounds from daylight to dark for forty dollars a month, the Cowboy has a very definite place in the march of western civilization.

C.H. Dodwell
(Honorary President)
Williams Lake Stampede

Williams Lake

Williams Lake is 500 kilometers due north of Vancouver, but no matter how you get there it is a trip west. At Cache Creek the Trans-Canada highway swings east, but the 97 continues on into Cariboo country. The claustrophobic closed-in feeling of the Fraser Canyon gives way, the sky opens up in sweeping, diffuse grandeur, revealing striking vistas and rolling burnt brown hills of the Interior Plateau. The west coast wetness is replaced by arid skies streaked with high, wispy clouds. It is a land of 4000 lakes; slate green, blissful blue, murky brown ponds and pools. Streams unhurried by thought or time snake through golden fields.

Daryl Palmantier is ready to ride at the Williams Lake Stampede.

Approaching Williams Lake I tune in to the Country All Hit radio station and get a hoe down of western music and the bubbly chatter from announcers and roving reporters gearing up for four days of Stampede fun and excitement. It soon becomes evident that there are many changes that have taken place since the last time I took in the Williams Lake Stampede, in the long-ago almost-forgotten summer of 1964. The town had hardly 2000 people when I left and has since grown to 11 222 (as of 1995) with those living in the surrounding district numbering 12 778, rounding the total off to a nice, even 24 000.

The parade always kicked off the then-three day event, and the highlight of it for me was the Indians, bedecked in feather headdresses, with their buckskin pants and embroidered shirts. Despite such outfits originating with the Plains Indians and not the local nations, it impressed me nonetheless.

Williams Lake has grown since those days, since the time I left swearing I would be extremely happy to never return. Concerts, outdoor music, a number of pancake breakfasts, logger sports, baseball and rugby tournaments, Main Street blocked off for sales and street entertainers have all improved the atmosphere. I found myself enjoying the ambiance of a town that had once had all the class and beauty of a broken ashtray with cigarette butts afloat in a scum of stale beer.

One thing that will never change is the impressive setting of the grounds in a natural bowl which opens to the south end, facing the lake. I was surprised and disappointed that the Indian teepees were no longer welcomed. As a youngster I was wowed by the sight of 100 or so of the beautiful white teepees, with the tall poles poking through the point of the conical shaped tents.

Another striking change, and I don't know when it took place, was the replacement of the old wooden stockades and grandstands. The new arrangement is much better for spectators, bringing them closer to the infield events, but a lack of space has made it impossible to run the full sized chuckwagons and now only the pony chucks race at Williams Lake.

But the history, and the stories, I was really interested in was the cowboys'. Leonard Palmantier was considered the best all-round cowboy in the Cariboo and was hard to beat in any event. There are many stories told about him, one being that he rode his horse into Stampede Hall to collect his prize. Today the fourth generation of Palmantiers are in the rodeo and I talked with grandson Daryl, who rides bulls.

Daryl sports a very light moustache, subtle and underplayed like the man himself. He is very quiet spoken, but when he got warmed up he talked about his well-known ancestor.

"He used to help me and my older brother Gerald," Daryl relates. "I heard stories that he used to put silver dollar coins under his boot in the stirrup when he'd ride a saddle bronc, and the coins would still be there when he finished."

Gerald, who was 12 years older than Daryl, had also been a big influence on the younger Palmantier, but sadly had passed away from cancer at the age of 37 in the preceding year. "He was probably the biggest influence on my bull riding," Daryl said softly. "He told me what I was doing wrong and what I should be doing."

One day, before the rodeo events got underway at Williams Lake, a moment's silence was held for Gerald, followed by the reading of the Cowboy's Prayer.

In all the years of the Williams Lake Stampede, there has only been one fatality at the rodeo. In 1932 Lloyd "Cyclone" Smith, who was known to be an outstanding cowboy, was arena manager and was acting as a pick-up man. A bronc had thrown his rider and was heading for a hole in the fence. Smith went to cut him off and the two horses collided. Smith's foot got caught in the stirrup and he was crushed beneath his horse when the two went down. He was taken unconscious to the hospital, where he later died.

Cyclone Smith was killed in the 13th Stampede and on his grave stone is enscribed: "Death is but a change of clothing as one steps across the border to a land of sunshine out of a land of snows" – Zabdiel.

Williams Lake has an excellent museum and there I found the following:

The significance of the Stampede to spectacular feats and heroic deeds.

Automobiles and white collars, morris chairs and Mah Jong have failed to do away with the irresistible fascination felt in the witnessing [of] exhibitions of dare-devil courage, where the principal pits his muscle and sinews and heart's blood against the cyclonic forces of nature, risking life and limb in a titanic contest against well-nigh overwhelming odds.

This is undoubtedly the immediate appeal which draws crowds annually to the Stampede. It explains the audible intake of breath heard on the grandstand as the rider mounts the half ton of steel and dynamite that is to hurl him to victory or defeat in the dust of the arena; it accounts for the smothered gasp when a rider falls; and for the exultant roar that flings to heaven when he "rides."

The Stampede, however, holds a deeper significance than this; an inner meaning felt only vaguely, subconsciously by the spectator, perhaps, but fraught with unspoken appeal. For in a subtle, intangible way, the Stampede is an atom of history – the history of the peopling of the West. It sums up for us the battle of the pioneer, forcing his way through the prairies, to the Pacific, blazing the way for the populations that have followed, conquering, one by one, terrific obstacles, bending the brute creation – all nature, in fact – to his service. It is the preservation of one page in the book of North America – the page of the Covered Wagon.

And it visualizes for us that lonely loveable supreme figure in the western migration, the COWBOY. Setting aside the ecstasies of romantic writers, the Cowboy remains, and always will remain, a type on which the mind dwells fondly. Keen eyed, careless, self-reliant, tuned to vast solitudes, calmly facing dangers and enduring hardships alone and unsung, lording it over horse and brute on the fringe of the world, taking life in one hand while rolling a cigarette in the other, sweating on round ups and freezing on feeding-grounds from daylight to dark for forty dollars a month, the Cowboy has a very definite place in the march of western civilization. Already most of his old ranges have been resigned to the truck farm and the dairy, and the Cowboy has folded his blankets and flitted. Only here and there, in some last stronghold of sagebrush and bunchgrass, does he still survive. But his day was a real and a vital one, and it only awaits some genius with a sense of values, some Kipling of the West to enshrine him for all time in the Literature of Canada.

This was by C.H. Dodwell, Esquire (Honorary President), 1924 Williams Lake Stampede Program Book.

Though the Williams Lake Stampede has changed since I enjoyed it as a grubby little scamp, it still has a mystique that makes it special.

The Party Begins

Although the cowboys have yet to arrive, Williams Lake is in a party mood. I ask around and most people agree that the best place to go for a drink is the Overlander, which is on the hill overlooking the Stampede grounds. "That's where the cowboys hang out," I'm told by more than one informed source.

I walk up the highway, and though it is late in the evening, the glow from the setting sun is still polishing the western sky with a golden glow. There is a decent sprinkling of attractive young ladies, which should have attracted cowboys, but to my disappointment, there are none. There wasn't a bull rider in sight. It was pointed out to me that the rodeo wasn't to start until 6:00 pm the next evening and was a short go round, so most of the rodeo people wouldn't be arriving until tomorrow. The other thing I didn't yet know was that the cowboys only came in for the one day of their event, and when it was finished they were off to the next rodeo as soon as they could change, so they weren't lingering about in the beer halls of Williams Lake where I could get a chance to talk to them.

The days of cowboys coming to the Williams Lake Stampede and staying for the duration are a thing of the past, except for the pony chuck wagon races, the exciting and somewhat dangerous Mountain Races and the Wild Horse Races (which fits into the category of "why the hell do they do that?").

Friday morning I drag my carcass out of bed and walk down to the Stampede grounds where there is already plenty of activity, even though the events don't officially get underway for several hours yet.

I walk into the Stampede Office located under the grandstand, where I explain to the lady behind the counter what I'm doing.

"Is it possible to get a press pass?" I ask.

Much to my surprise she is very pleasant and replies, "It sure is."

No long explanations required, no grilling on her part, no bouncing me from one person to the next, just a laminated 1997 Williams Lake Media pass. I was expecting similar treatment to what I had received in Luxton, but the attitudes couldn't have been more different.

"Can I go down by the chutes and talk to the cowboys?"

"Yes," she says. "Just be real careful when you cross the track," she admonishes me before I have the chance to do anything wrong.

I smile. Was she there about 35 years ago when I had bolted across the track just before a race was to begin? The guy controlling the gate had said it was okay to go, but the announcer blared out, "Get that kid off the track!" In addition to feeling every eye in the place on me, I knew that Mom would be fuming. I wasn't wrong. I really got what for when I joined her in the stands.

Now, I feel elated. This is the break I need.

From the Stampede grounds I go to the Boitano Mall (named for a local rancher) for breakfast. Fortified with eggs, bacon, sausages, toast and hash browns, and about 10 cups of coffee, I walk down the hill to the rodeo grounds. The pony chucks are running and I wait on the slope above the track for the all-clear signal then dash across the track and walk into the infield where the parking lot is filled with trailers, campers, cars and pickup trucks. Cowboys sleep with their feet up on the doors, some are changing their clothes, children scamper about. Old friends who haven't seen each other in some time are greeting each other.

In the pens there is one bull in with a half dozen horses. The bull stands in one corner, by himself, looking warily at the horses who bunch up in the opposite corner. I sit on a long log bench and a dozen cowboys sit at the other end, chatting. I feel some empathy with the bull, though the analogy would have been better if it was one horse in a pen full of bulls.

I wander about. There are two cowboys getting their gear from the back of a pick-up truck. I ask them what event they're in. They ride saddle broncs. I am surprised at their shyness. They are gentle young men and not what I would have expected from saddle bronc riders. There is no aggressiveness, no swagger, just two very soft-spoken men. Cody Meston and his traveling partner, Justin Asped, are from Tees, Alberta. "I hope we get in the money," Cody says. "We need it to get back home."

I watch the events and wander around behind the chutes where the number of cowboys slowly grows.

Tony Gregg is at the microphone keeping the audience, pretty sparse this early in the afternoon, entertained. The pony chucks are running. ". . . he's a pretty big man," Tony says of the driver of the rig that is sponsored by Tim Horton's Donuts. "He eats more than donuts. He's big enough to burn diesel."

The cowboys are stretching out. Equipment is hung up on the pen rails. A pair of Wrangler blue jeans hangs from the rails, the shape of their owner evident in their form.

I walk back and forth in aimless patterns, passing Cody and Justin, who've got their black cowboy hats down low over their eyes. Their large belt buckles are prominent. They've got chaps with their initials on them, and of course cowboy boots. Not shiny new boots, but well worn boots with spurs that jingle softly when they walk.

They are quiet, subdued, as they wait for their event to come up.

"I hate this waiting," Cody says.

Everyone hates it. I can feel the mood in all the cowboys. The tension. Not exaggerated tension, not high strung tension, just that edge, that wanting to get on with things. They are anxious to get out in the arena and get the job done.

Saddle bronc riders Justin Asped (left) and Cody Meston of Tees, Alberta.

Finally, the saddle bronc riding comes and the riders are into the chutes. When Cody's turn comes up, Tony Gregg tells the Friday night audience that Cody is now number four in Canada, but earlier in the year was number one. He scores a 63 and Justin a 54. I would never have guessed that this quiet, unassuming young man was one of the best in his sport. There was nothing in his attitude that said, "I'm good, and I'll show you how good I am."

Cody and Justin are laughing, talking and grinning when they come out of the arena. Their mood has changed completely and Cody comes over and talks so fast I have a hard time keeping up with him as I jot notes.

"One time everyone before us had No Time," he says. "I could've come at least second if

I'd just stayed on my horse, but he went forward on me and I got No Time. You think about that for the next 12 hours," his hand indicates the direction, "as you're going down the road to the next place."

"You came off limping," I edge a few words in.

"Yeah, I kinda got kicked when I came off. The horses can be just as hard on you as the bulls. The bulls'll try and step on you, they'll get their hooves up and try to get you. But the horse won't. They're hard on you in other ways. The saddle broncs can be really hard on you if you are loose in the saddle. It bangs you around a lot.

"Some of the older guys can jump off and land on their feet," he's watching me write. "It's tough to do. I tried to do it and I landed on my head." He doesn't pauses to let us enjoy the image. "The other thing is we always wear loose boots." He shows me how loose his cowboy boots are, which contrasts with the bull riders, some of whom bind theirs up tight. "If you get hung up they come off. I got 250 stitches when I got hung up one time. Another time I got 300 stitches in my leg when a horse tore my calf off. The only bones I've broken were my nose and my finger when I was helping someone in the chutes."

You can see the adrenaline is pumping. Their eyes are clearer, their smiles wider and they are feeling the rush that keeps them going back for another ride when they know the danger, when they are down to their last dollar, and when there are a lot of other things their families would like them to be doing.

Is there a difference between bull riders and saddle bronc riders? Not a lot, but some. A significant some. The level of danger is higher for bull riders. Horses don't go after their riders, they will avoid trying to step on them, even when they are bucking like mad and the cowboy is holding his hands over his head as he cringes in the dust amidst those pounding, lethal hooves. A bull can go after the man the moment he lowers himself onto his back in the chute and he doesn't give up on him until he is out of the infield. You don't walk away from a bull, you run, because he can do you damage walking.

Waiting for the bull riding event to begin, I feel like the lone bull in the corral with horses, but once I start talking to the riders all the barriers came down and they talk at length about what they do. Why are they so open? I don't know at first. I thought they were simply being their natural friendly selves, which I'm sure they were. But there is one other element which should have been evident to me; it is the very reason why I picked bull riders to write about – so very little has been written about them. They want their story told.

They participate in a sport that requires a high degree of skill, they spend years developing their skills and take a terrific physical pounding doing it. For their efforts they get less recognition and money than a man who swings at a golf ball, swats at a hockey puck or kicks a soccer ball. Very few people understand their sport and those who do are limited, to a large degree, to the participants. Few others really know what happens during those few seconds that the man is on the beast. There are rodeo people who know the sport, and all the difficulties that it entails, but outside of them not many know what is required to stay on a bull for the eight seconds.

There are fans who can appreciate a good ride, but they know little about the technique, and the physical and the mental attributes that go into making a good bull rider. In the following days and weeks, I was to learn a lot about the sport, but it took a lot of tough digging, because often the cowboys themselves couldn't explain the process. Some of it was self-evident.

The attributes that make a good bull rider are the same qualities that make a good competitor in any sport. Focus, determination, persistence, practice and dedication. Then there are the intangibles. Those things inside a man that makes him more determined, that makes him more persistent, so that he dedicates himself to a greater degree than anyone else.

What makes a man a good bull rider? Any cowboy will tell you.

Cowboy Christmas

"This is what they call Cowboy Christmas," the voice of Tony Gregg echoes off the hills that enclose the Williams Lake Stampede grounds. "On this Canada Day long weekend a cowboy can go to as many as five rodeos. If he has been having a mediocre season up until now, this weekend can turn it around for him. Or, if he has a bad weekend, it might put him out of contention."

The bull riders wait under the awning that is stretched over half a dozen picnic tables. This is their change room, out in the open. They have been doing it this way for so long they think nothing of it. Few of the rodeos and bull-o-ramas have anything resembling what most athletes would consider adequate change rooms. Some rodeos have a trailer or small room where they can change. Often they choose not to use them.

Imagine Wayne Gretzky having to change into his hockey equipment in the concourse under the stands!

A *Calgary Sun* reporter went to the Strathmore bull-o-rama, and after observing them getting ready to ride, wrote about the bull riders as warriors, getting ready to do battle.

I never got that sense. One cowboy putting on his flack jacket turned and said to me, "It's my armor." However, the impression the cowboys gave to me, one they wanted to convey, was that they are professional athletes. They compete against an opponent who is physically much stronger, but they not only respect their opponents, they like them. And the ranker the bull, the greater the admiration. They are not battling an enemy they want to destroy.

No question, they do recognize the danger, and there is a certain amount of bravado in some of them, but most it was the quiet determination to do a good job that was the dominant attitude.

Glen Keeley is one of the best riders on the Canadian rodeo circuit. In 1989 he won the Canadian Championship and in mid-1997, he was third in earnings. He is the third oldest in a family of ranchers that began with his grandparents. His older brother Clayton has been to the Canadian finals and David "got his education paid through riding in the rodeo."

"I am probably the worst rider in my family," Glen tells me as we sit at the picnic tables. "But I guess I've got too hard a head, so I keep going."

Glen, like most bull riders, is quiet spoken, but his words go right to where he lives. "I like this lifestyle. Bull riding is different than any sport I've played. There are a lot of variables to it. When it works, it seems pretty easy. When it's not working it seems pretty damned hard."

He is wearing a white cowboy hat, and his lanky, strong face is constantly warmed by a wry grin. He squints against the dust and the light and the thoughts that bring back strong memories.

"Nervous? Yeah, but I try to turn that into aggression. As I get older I can't get worked up for it like I used to. You get yourself up for it like you would for a hockey game. When I get a little nervous I get revved up, but you can't overdo it, you've got to turn it into aggression."

Is this weekend a Cowboy Christmas or is it a holiday they can't afford?

"When I leave here," Keeley states. "I'm going to drive to Meadow Lake, that's about 12 to 13 hours. Then I go to Swift Current. I'm going to Ponoka and Airdrie. This run alone is going to cost me $2300-$2500. That's my break even. It's $3000 if you win here in Williams Lake. Living in Alberta is pretty good because it is three to four hours to get to the rodeos. It is more difficult on the guys in BC because they've got further to go. In the winter I go down to the States."

There are no guarantees in the world of rodeo. About 16 bull riders come to Williams Lake vying for the top prize, and only one man is going to win it. There are smaller winnings, but the further down the list you get, the more difficult it is to reach that break even point. In addition, the contestants all pay for the privilege of participating in this sport. Entrance fees vary from rodeo to rodeo.

1989 Canadian Bull Riding Champion, Glen Keeley of Nanton, Alberta.

The riders ride for the jazz, for the high it gives them. They take a long time preparing for their ride, and in eight seconds or less, it is all over. What do they do to settle down afterwards?

"Well, that depends on the ride," Glen muses. "If I didn't ride good then I'm pretty worked up."

On this, the first day of the Stampede, the rodeo starts at 6:00 pm, and though the sun won't set for some time yet, a scud of black clouds dims the light. There is a lot going on in the arena, but the cowboys seem unaware of it. They are focussing their minds on their ride. Some go through the motions, their free hand in the air, they grip an imaginary rope and ride a bull that takes them exactly where they want to go. Which is seldom the same trip

Bull rider Jim Leatherberry – the Gordie Howe of bull riding.

they take when they leave the chute.

Jim Leatherberry is a rare specimen. He is 46 years old in a sport where the top men are in their mid-20s or *younger*. The competitors in the other rodeo events generally average ten years longer in the profession than the bull riders. Leatherberry is the exception.

Leatherberry bounces up and down on his toes. If he put this effort into forward motion, he'd make it to Meadow Lake and back. His black cowboy hat is pulled halfway down his forehead over a ruddy face with a few small scars. His teeth are yellowed from years of chewing tobacco. Except for the crows' feet around his eyes, there is a tautness to his skin which gives him a placid expression that contrasts with the quiet intensity of his eyes. I have the feeling that he would just as soon not talk to me, but he does. And I take a great deal of his time probing into things he might well have thought I shouldn't bother with, but he doesn't complain.

Things have changed a great deal from when Jim began bull riding in the early '60s. Ronnie Rossen was the World Champion in 1961 and again in '65 and was one of the guys Jim emulated. But it was different then. "There's a lot more money now than there was then," Jim notes.

When Rossen won the World Championship in 1961, his earnings for that year were $13 392. When Terry West won the Worlds in 1996 he rode off with $125 425. Tuff Hedeman has won over one million dollars riding bulls. The big money is in the U.S. When the National Finals Rodeo was held in Las Vegas, a total of $3 218 292 was paid out for all events in 1996. The Calgary Stampede, largest in Canada, paid out $211 680 and ranked only 13th in payouts in 1996.

"If you hang in there you're going to make a lot of money. You can make a damn good living at it," Jim asserts. "You win the Worlds and you're into good money. There are a lot of events that are for bull riders only. So there is more money in the sport. But the great thing about bull riding is that you get to be your own boss. You do your own thing. You've got nobody telling you what to do."

He listens thoughtfully to the questions, and he isn't bouncing up and down while we talk. As he does when riding bulls, he focuses on the job at hand.

"The sport is much better organized now than it was," Jim states. "It's much more professional than when I started. They've got rules now. They used to cheat a little, but now everything is computer drawn. When I started they'd give you whatever (bull) they wanted. Now it is as fair as it gets. I like it better now than when I first started."

Not only has the organization changed, so have the bulls. "They're a lot ranker now. You get to know them pretty good," there is a warm tone to his voice. "If you don't know them there is always someone around who does. I like Kodiac and Cliff Hanger is supposed to be a good bull. Everybody's got a few bulls you don't like. There are a few around I don't like. They buck, but they're eliminators. They'll hurt you."

Kodiak is Kodiak Copenhagen, Bull of the Year in 1996. Wayde Joyal was the only one to ride him that year out of the 19 times he bucked at Pro Rodeos.

Like all the other cowboys, Leatherberry respects his opponent. "They ain't dumb," he says of the bulls. "I like a bull that bucks hard and turns back. And you've gotta be moving too. If you just sit there, they're going to throw you off. You can be riding good for six seconds then suddenly they'll go ahead and rise up and throw your ass off. On a good bull the time goes fast. If they don't buck, it seems like a long time."

Jim is an old hand at the sport, but if he knows what it is that makes him a good enough bull rider to hang in there for so long, he isn't telling. "I get on and hang on and hope I ride right," is all he says about his technique.

Keeping free of injuries is one of the keys to longevity for bull riders. But an injury that might make lesser mortals reluctant to get back in the game are routine for bull riders.

"I've been hurt," says Leatherberry, "but not bad enough to put me out for any length of time. I've been pretty lucky." We talk about other things, then when I ask him about specific injuries, he admits to having his "legs broke a few times" along with ribs, his jaw and his arm. Those are not considered serious injuries.

Cowboys stretch and try to keep loose before their ride. They sit at the benches and chat, and they don't pay any attention to what is going on in the infield. The sweet scent of manure is airborne in the persistent breeze that whips up the dust and dirt the stock is kicking about.

Daren Tuftin, the rodeo clown, comes out from the in-field and sits down and has a cigarette while waiting for his next performance. I chat with him for awhile, then have a look at the events in the arena. There is a good noisy crowd.

Jim is bouncing up and down on his toes. Looks a little self conscious when I glance his way.

Photographers stand on railings, ladies rush about with sheets of paper and an air of importance. The Stampede Queen and her Princesses go by selling 50/50 tickets. The crowd buzzes and horses bang about in the stockades. The bull pen is located next to the picnic tables where the cowboys lounge about. The bulls bellow and kick up dirt and bang the steel rails and the non-stop patter of Tony Gregg overlays all the other noise. I thought that the cowboys were particularly quiet, but that isn't so. It's just that I can't hear them talking over the clamor of the rodeo.

I go back and talk to Jim some more and he says he would like to continue to ride for a few more years, "You can make a damn good living at it," he says. Having won Calgary "a few years ago" certainly beefed up his bank account. At the end of the season he plans to "drink a little beer and mess around a little bit. I don't do much," he says with a bit of a smile.

But now there are still many bulls to ride and miles to travel before the end of the season. "Can I talk to you after you ride?" I ask, hoping he will be able to explain what happened.

"Sure," he nods.

Twelve-year-old Jordie Nash of Blackie, Alberta, is getting ready to steer ride. When I ask him why he does this, he responds in a quiet mature manner. "I come from a rodeo family and I just want to carry on the tradition. I thought that it looked like fun. I wanted to try it." His father rode bulls, but he broke his leg and had to quit. Getting ready for his ride, Jordie goes about his business in the same quiet manner the pros do.

Shane Mills of Pink Mountain, B.C., is also carrying on a family tradition. "I grew up on a ranch, so I guess it's in my blood and I like the challenge." His older brother, Daryl, won the World Championships and $105 000 in 1994.

I ask Shane if he remembers his first ride.

Young steer riders take their sport as seriously as the bull riders take theirs.

He smiles, "Yes, but there's not much to tell. The bull was pretty good. He jerked me around, spun me around, hung me up and flung me to the ground." His smile widens, "It was a pretty good rush, I thought."

Glen Keeley also started at an early age, "It's a lifestyle," he explains. "I grew up around animals. It's not like some city kids getting on a bull. I know the animals."

I take a picture of Daren trying to stuff his dog Buster into duffle bag. Buster doesn't think this is a good part of the act and refuses to co-operate. Daren is supposed to be in the infield and Tony Gregg is covering for him while Buster fights incarceration.

Once he's out there, I turn my attention to the infield, "And you've got to get a long little doggie," Daren is saying over the wireless mike on his headphones. "What's that?" Tony Gregg asks in disbelief.

"You've got to get a long little doggie," and with that the suitcase is opened and Buster squeezes out of the duffle bag and runs out of the infield, to the laughter and applause of the audience.

When Daren trots off with all his props he says, "That's the first time I've done that trick with him."

Which explains Buster's reluctance to get into the bag.

Daren sports a battered white cowboy hat that is pulled down low to a backward question mark between his eyebrows. He has white patches around his eyes that come down his cheek. Of course his nose is red. His lopsided smile is made more lopsided by a missing tooth. "His big trick is when I shoot him, and he dies. In fact, it's his only trick."

The clowns and the bullfighters cluster in a group and don't interact much with the cowboys.

"I've never been hooked bad," says bullfighter Mark Nichols.

"How do you get hooked good?" another bullfighter asks sarcastically.

The bulls are being moved into the chutes. Some move quickly and without much fuss, while others don't like being told where to go and they protest noisily at this intrusion into their lives.

Jim Leatherberry continues to jump and down.

Another rider walks by and says, "Good luck, Jim."

"You too," he replies sincerely to the man he's competing against for the prize money.

The tension increases. More guys are going through imaginary, preparatory rides. Looking down at their bull, holding their rope, waving their free hand. Their moment in the limelight is rapidly approaching.

"DO YOU WANNA SEE SOME BULL RIDING TONIGHT!?"

A lukewarm response comes from the crowd.

"DO YOU WANNA SEE SOME BULL RIDING TONIGHT?" Tony Gregg shouts out the question again and a roar goes up from the crowd. The music is pumped up, *"We will, we will, ROCK YOU!"*

The crowd begins to sing and clap and stomp with the throbbing music.

"This is the MOST DANGEROUS SPORT IN NORTH AMERICA," Gregg tells the world. "As recently voted on by the sports writers of North America. It is not a question of *if* they are going to be hurt, but *when*."

The crowd is ready. Billy Jones is lowering himself onto No Respect. The bull leaps out, turns, Billy is hanging tight, but it is a rough ride and he sticks to score a 78.

Jim Leatherberry is next. I want him to do well. I'm pulling for him, but his bull takes no more than a few steps, leaps, twists and tosses him to the dirt. I feel bad. I hoped he would do well. When he comes out of the infield, his head is down and his face is dark, so I don't bother him. Later, someone tells me that he's had a hand injury and hasn't ridden all spring. It's going to take him awhile to get back in form.

Behind the chutes Glen Keeley is keeping loose. In apparent anger he slams down a rope at the feet of another cowboy. Then he laughs. Guys are taped up, got their chaps and vests on, they slap their arms, they're ready to go. The bulls are good, giving the riders a tough time.

The action really heats up when the bullfighting competition gets underway. This is a relatively new event at Stampedes and allows the bullfighters to show off their skills. These guys seem really crazy, facing down the bull alone. They get out in the arena with a bull and a clown in the barrel. They get the bull's attention and when the bull charges the bullfighter leaps to the side, the bull's horns passing closely. The closer the pass, the higher the score. Then the bullfighter gets the bull to knock the barrel around, with the clown inside.

When the bullfighting is over, the three fighters are one point apart, but Mark Nichols is not pleased at all. "Fuckin' judges up here," he snarls. "I can't fuckin' believe it. I can't believe the three of us were one point apart."

Ricky Ticky Wanchuck was the man in the barrel and he comes out of the infield breathing hard. "He knocked the shittin' wind out of me," he puffs, breathing deeply. He looks at me from behind his grease paint, but it is not hard to read his emotions. "He broke my feather." He holds up his hat with a large feather that is bent in the middle.

"Now that is going a little too far," I respond.

He smiles, "You can do a lot of things to me, but don't break my feather."

"You like this? You like getting in there with the bulls?"

He looks at me like I'm a little crazy. "I must like it. I've been doing it for 20 years." He catches his breath, straightens out the feather. "I live for them. The rodeos. It gives me a chance," he stops, "Here I'm like one of the cowboys. I come in and do my act. I'm not out on the highway somewhere pulling my rig."

When the bullfighting is over, the second half of the bull riding goes on, but it is delayed while the cowboy tries to get on a bull that doesn't want any part of this show. The bull finally falls down in the chute, he doesn't want to play today. The cowboy is pulled off by the men working the chutes. After five minutes of trying to get the rider set, they give up on the bull and let him take another one.

"Careful, cowboy," the announcer advises while the cowboy is trying to get on this rank bull.

"Why do they do it?" Gregg asks rhetorically. "We don't know why they do it, but we're glad that they do."

"Yeah, because they make us money," says one of the bullfighters.

When the bull riding is over, the stands clear out quickly.

Later, in a quiet local pub, I meet Ed Allain. "I'm just having so much fun. I can't believe it. I just love it. I love the rodeo," he says. "I was born in the wrong province. I'm from New Brunswick. I've wanted to be a cowboy since I was five years old. I like to sketch, so I was sketching horses all day. I spent the whole day at the Stampede. It is an incredible place. Wow! Like you won't find anywhere else like it. It's . . . it's so . . ." he gets lost for words.

"I went to the rodeo at Cloverdale, but it was like being in a strip mall. This is my first time in Williams Lake. Williams Lake is the . . ." he's at a loss for words to adequately describe the Cowtown.

"It's the real thing," I suggest.

He readily agrees. "There's a real special feeling here. The bulls – wow! I went to the Cloverdale rodeo and only one guy stayed on the bulls. Like tonight, I've been watching the bulls for a week, and tonight I saw some of them being ridden."

I also talk rodeo with a middle-aged woman.

"You here for the Stampede?"

"Yeah."

"Me too. I really like the rodeo."

"I'm writing about the bull riders."

"You're a bull rider?"

"No, I'm writing about the bull riders," I very carefully pronounced 'writing.'

"Oh, that's interesting," she asks me a few questions, then says, "You know what you have to do. You have to ride a bull to learn what it's like."

"No I don't," I replied. "These guys are professional athletes. They don't just go out and leap on a bull. Most of them start when they're very young and grow into it. They train for it, and learn the sport."

"No, you really should ride them," she urges.

"Not a chance," I reply.

The Williams Lake Stampede.

Mark Nichols challenges the bull at the bullfighting competition at the Williams Lake Stampede.

Bullfighting competition at the Williams Lake Stampede.

Good bulls make good bull fighters.

Ricky Ticky Wanchuk
Rodeo Clown

"Bullfighting is a really tough job. If it wasn't for them there'd be a lot more guys hurt."

Jim Leatherberry
Bull Rider

Don't Make It Look Too Easy

There are a couple of events at the Williams Lake Stampede that aren't held at every rodeo. One is the mountain race, which had originally started higher up the mountain than what is run today. It is still exciting as the racers go at full gallop along a stretch that runs along the hill then plunge at heart stopping speed down the steep slope to the race track where they thunder to the finish line in front of the grandstand.

The chariot races are also characterized by a fierce competitiveness in a sport that not many participate in. The chariots, a small two wheeled vehicle about the same size as Ben Hur's chariot, but without the Roman flourishes, is pulled by a two horse team. The start is like the chuck wagon races, where the chariots have to be maneuvered around a couple of barrels, and more than one will flip over, sending the cowboy tumbling into the dirt. He'll retrieve his hat, right the chariot and get back into the race.

Roman helmets are replaced by cowboy hats, armored plates by flannel shirts, metal shin protectors and sandals by cowboy boots. The Romans might have learned some lessons in competitiveness as these cowboys urge their charges on to greater speeds as they attempt to leave the others in their dust. These races are a lot of fun and add to the unique flavor of the Williams Lake Stampede.

The boys' steer riding takes place early in the program. "And now . . ." Tony Gregg is stirring up the already noisy crowd. "The great stepping stone event . . . the boys' steering riding. These young cowboys get their training on the steers, then they go to the bulls . . ."

The boys can hang on to the rope with both hands, and that's what most of them do, most of the time. Aaron Pierce gets on his mount and has a good ride to the bell. When the claxon sounds, Aaron is having so much fun he lets go of the rope with one hand and waves it in the air like the bull riders. He goes a few more leaps and bounds on the energetic steer, to the cheers of the crowd, then executes a rough dismount. The crowd loves it, and shows their appreciation. He walks slowly out of the infield to the compliments of the cowboys.

The clowns and bullfighters are in their group at the edge of the picnic tables. The cowboys are clustered in small groups and they seem more relaxed than yesterday's competitors. There's a bit of horsing around, slapping each other, laughing and talking. This is Williams Lake, after all, one of the highlights of the season.

I chat with Ricky and Mark, who I'd met the day before, and today Mark is in a much better mood. It turned out that he was the winner of the previous day's bull fighting, as the announcer had the names wrong.

"I was a little pissed," Mark says.

"Did you hear the one about the guy who goes into the bar and says to the bartender, 'Give me 10 of your most expensive drinks'," a bull rider is telling the story. "'You'd better make them doubles', the guy says. So the bartender pours out 10 shooters and the guy drinks them down one after the other as fast as he can. 'Wow,' the bartender says. 'You really drank those quickly.' 'Well, you would too if you had what I've got,' says the customer. 'Oh,' says the bartender, backing away a bit. 'What've you got?' 'About 75¢,' replies the customer."

One cowboy laughs delightedly. "You've got to tell that to . . ." he goes off to get another cowboy and the story is repeated.

Daren Tuftin goes into the arena dressed up in a poor imitation of a poor imitation of Elvis Presley. He's playing air guitar to one of the King's rock hits. I'm chatting with Ricky Ticky Wanchuk when suddenly there is one hell of an explosion, guitar and clown go flying in different directions. Daren is flat on his back in the dirt.

The first aid corps rush into action carrying a stretcher. They run past the prostrate clown, put the guitar on the stretcher and rush off.

Mark walks past, "He's going to blow his leg off one of these days. I watched him getting ready and he put a big wad of powder into the pipe and he taped it up real good."

Which is what made the real good bang.

I chat with the soft spoken Daryl Palmantier. When he's not riding, he works in the bush, logging, which he needs to do because bull riding isn't making him a great deal of money. Like many of the riders. There is big money for the guys at the top, but the man sitting next to the money winner might be down to his last dollar and trying to decide whether to use that to get to the next rodeo or to go home. They usually choose the rodeo.

"I've been doing this for 5 or 6 years," Daryl says. "It hasn't been going too well lately, but I expect things to pick up here pretty quick. I make about $5-6000 a year. I've always got hurt or gone home broke." By the end of this weekend he's only made a bit more than $1600 and was 23rd in winnings. Kelly Armstrong is way out in front for season earnings with $7584.72. Not exactly big bucks for the beating they take on the back of the bulls.

How long can a guy keep going like this?

"I don't know," Daryl looks down. "I hope it'll come together someday."

Why?

"I don't know," his eyes search the ground. "It's something I always wanted to do. It's fun when you stay on. You get a pretty good rush."

When I finish talking with Daryl, I'm sitting by myself. Clint Ostrem is sitting further down and leans forward. "Didn't I see you down in Luxton?"

"Yeah," I say. "How's it going?"

"It's off and on," he says. "I broke my hand this spring when I landed on it. I keep coming back and trying it. It's good now."

The cowboys downplay the emotion they feel when they get on the bull. Few of them would admit to being scared, but some do say that some bulls make them nervous. They all agree that if you're thinking too much about it you shouldn't be doing the job. Whatever their emotions, you can see the tension on their face just before they give the nod and the chute flies open. Often they grit their teeth, their faces tense as they get set to experience what they consider to be the greatest of all rushes.

The riders are focussed once they get into the chute. There is a great air of seriousness as they wrap the rope around their gloved hand. Tightly. Slowly, making sure it is exactly right. Their handlers are trying to build their confidence, constantly calling them cowboy – reminding them of their heritage, their responsibility to not tarnish the image, reminding them of their uniqueness as a member of a small and elite group.

The rider's head is down, eyes down, the bull bangs about in the chute trying to mash the cowboys legs. This is a most dangerous moment in bull riding. More riders get hurt here than in the arena. The cowboy grits his teeth and he goes, hoping for eight seconds to glory.

1996 Canadian Bull Riding Champion Jay Manning prepares for his next ride.

One bull doesn't want to go back into the anonymity of the pens and he eludes the cowboys for a long time. "Ricky," says the rodeo announcer, "Go pull his tail. You'll get a kick out of it."

Finally they release two more bulls into the arena. One trots up to the showboater, butts heads with him and then trots off to the pens with the first bull following closely.

Daryl Palmantier has a pretty good ride and gets a decent 75 points, but the crowd thinks he should have scored higher and their boos and jeers let the judges know how they feel. But the mark doesn't change.

"The bull wasn't that great today," Daryl tells me. "You've got to spur them. The judges sometimes take points away from you if you make it look too easy." The highest Daryl has ever scored is a very impressive 90.

Clint scores 78, putting him ahead of Daryl and a shot at some money, as Williams Lake generously pays to 12 positions. Clint packs his kit, chats up a young lady who's standing on the other side of the fence.

"I'm not pushing it as hard this year," Clint says, about the bulls, not the girls. "I'm just staying in Canada and maybe I'll go to 35 rodeos and 15 to 20 bull ridings. The bull ridings are really good for us because there is no entrance fee at all, and there is more money for us. It seems to be what the people want, and the sponsors like to get into it."

The line between audacity and insanity is thin. In rodeo it's an inch wide – the thickness of a bull rider's rope. It's a tough but infinitely fragile line separating disaster from glory.

Don Wise
Chute That Horse

There's No Pain Like It

Sunday morning people are up early, up earlier than I was, and lined up for the pancake breakfasts. I decide to give the motel coffee shop a try.

Over breakfast I read a supplement put out by one of the local papers, which has a story about Gerald James, a bull rider from nearby Red Stone. He was nearly killed by a bull in Calgary in 1991. The bull had stepped on him. Guaranteed not to do a body any good whatsoever.

Down at the grounds I wander around, passing time, as it is still early in the day. I find a place near the chutes to watch the infield events. Shelly Green is standing next to me, and she admits to knowing a lot of cowboys. "It doesn't seem to matter what happens to them," she says. "They always seem to get back on again."

"Are they crazy?"

"It's a fine line," she laughs. She was married to a cowboy for "a long time" and is going to marry another.

As the events progress, more cowboys gather so I go to the picnic tables where they are congregating. I say hello to the guy sitting next to me and ask him his name.

"Gerald James," he replies.

"I was just reading about you," I'm surprised at the coincidence. "I was reading about how you nearly got killed in Calgary."

He nods.

"Was the story accurate?"

"Yeah, they did a good story on me," he replies.

"Can you tell me what happened?"

"Yeah," he's interrupted by his daughter who's flitting about then he says, "He was a good bull. I've been on him when I won a rodeo." He then explains what happened in Calgary. "He jumped out of the chute coming around to the right and caught me a bit outside and he threw me off. I came down ahead of him and landed on my back. He stepped right on my chest. From the time he stepped on me until I was being operated on was 20 minutes. I had a lacerated liver, a punctured lung, broken ribs and a bruised heart."

The flack jackets didn't come in until the following year, and they would have done a lot to lessen his injuries.

Perhaps what is most amazing is that the following year Gerald made a great comeback.

"That happened in July," he continues, "for two-three months I couldn't do too much. But then I got into a good workout program and by March I was riding again. I went hard that year and made it to the Canadian finals."

"Were you thinking about your last ride when you got on again?"

"No, I had to block that right out. When I went to Calgary again, I was nervous, and I got the same bull and rode him to a 74. If you start young enough, you get the basics so when you get in there you just think about what you are going to do, and you do it. I just thought about riding. I rode for years before that happened, it was an unusual thing and wouldn't be likely to happen again."

Injuries seemed to be the topic of the day. Rick Henderson tells me about his more serious injuries collected in 15 years of being a bull jockey. He had his biceps torn off six years ago, shattered his elbow and shattered his cheek bone last year.

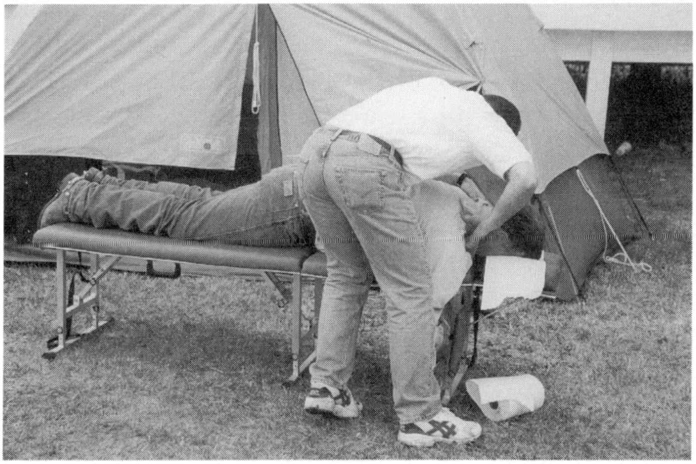

Sports medicine is helping the cowboys compete at their sport for a longer time.

Henderson, at 5 foot 11 inches, is tall for a bull rider. Most of them seem to be between 5'7" and 5'9", 140-160 lbs. Most of the big guys are into steer wrestling. He has a long, lean face and a black moustache, another rarity in the generally clean shaven fraternity.

"You're a fool if you think you're not going to be hurt," Rick states. "No one likes to think about it, but it does happen. And most guys know that they are going to go back in there because sports medicine has improved so much. It's God's gift to rodeo. If you've got a good therapist, he'll get you back in there as soon as you can."

Sports medicine has greatly helped the sport, but the rider's attitude towards conditioning has also improved.

Jack Johansen and his four brothers are among Canada's best bull riders. Jack now operates a highly successful bull riding school in Strathmore. "We did all the weight training and conditioning before it became the thing to do," he says. "As sports medicine gets better, it is going to keep the guys riding longer, but they've got to keep in shape. We emphasize a lot of upper body work, bike riding and weight lifting. Not heavy weights, but multiple weights because they have to keep flexible. You don't want hard muscles, you have to keep flexible. They have to stretch a lot, keep loose. A cowboy needs all the abilities that other athletes need, except for perhaps endurance; they are only in there for eight seconds, so stamina is not a high priority."

Bull riders approach their sport in the same manner that all professional athletes do. They develop their body to meet the demands they are going to face in competition. They all keep in shape, but they do it in different ways. Some do it through their jobs. Many work on ranches where tossing bales of hay around keeps them fit. Others work in trucking, logging, construction and on the oil rigs, and really don't need to do a great deal else to keep the muscles toned. Some work out in the gym, in weight rooms and do road work.

Conditioning is not only important for the eight seconds in the arena, but Johansen asserts that it is important for all aspects of the sport and that if a guy is not in shape, the travelling is going to wear him down. "Two days on the road and they're toast," he says.

Chad Wakefield has been in hospital "more times than I can remember" and the pounding is not only shortening his career but limiting the time he is able to spend riding in his prime time.

Lonny Corbet, who rode semi-pro for six years, suffered a serious injury, and the financial repercussions that can go with it. "I got hurt in '92 when the flack jackets were just coming in. I wouldn't've been as badly hurt had I been wearing one. The bull tossed me and then stepped on my chest. I

It's not a big problem, the cowboy is assured, after having a rough ride at the Williams Lake Stampede.

leapt straight up, I didn't even use my hands to help me up and I jumped over a six foot fence and I saw this guy there and I said to him, 'I'm in trouble.' I knew exactly what had happened. Then I passed out. My chest was so swollen my heart was shifting. They had to cut through my ribs to operate on it. I was in Olds and when they got me to Calgary the doctors there couldn't believe what they had done.

"It was the most painful experience I've ever had. There's no pain like it. I was in such bad shape I had to get the nurses to help me move."

The other pain was that at the time he didn't have Blue Cross, and the Association he was a member of had less coverage than what they do today.

"This happened up in Olds and they had to transport me to Calgary, it was February 4, my Mom's birthday, and it was foggy so they couldn't fly. The ambulance bill was $12 000, which I had to pay. The ambulance people were pretty understanding and they let me do payments. It took me a couple of years to pay it off."

There are numerous stories about cowboys being seriously injured in this sport, but even when they are not being stomped or hooked by a bull, the rider's bodies are taking a pounding. Muscles and ligaments are being stretched, muscles take a beating. They all have scars, cuts, bruises and scrapes and the jolting of the bull and the sudden stop at the end of a fall rattle their bones and brains. It wears them down, which is a prime reason their careers average ten years less than those in the other events.

"When you've taken a lot of pounding," Dave Leader points out, "You start to lose your edge and you don't ride so well. You've got to keep in shape so your muscles can take the strain. You're not trying to get big, you just want to keep your muscles toned."

Sometimes the cowboys are knocked out and suffer concussions. Both Clint Ostrem and Jay Manning have been knocked out "six or seven times."

"I got knocked out one time," Jay Manning relates, "and then I went out and spent a half hour in the parking lot looking for my truck." He pauses. "I'd been driving a car for two months."

"I started riding when I was 15," says Clint Ellis.

"I was 13," puts in Derek Adams.

Bernie Bowe, now 37, started when he was 16.

Derek Adams, who'd just turned 22, is a talker and a story teller. "I started too early," he speaks loudly. "I'd rode 2000 bulls by the time I was 20. You really take a pounding. I was beat up like I was 25." Everyone laughs, but he doesn't see the joke. "I've broken my leg three times, my wrist has been operated on twice." He's sitting on the corner of the bench looking around at the guys. "It wears you down upstairs."

Kelly McEwan, now 30 years old, has been riding for 15 years, but is one of the fortunate ones not to have suffered a serious injury. That doesn't mean he hasn't been in a few wrecks. "I took a hook one time," he laughs. "He rolled me around pretty good. I was just in the wrong place. I've had a few broken legs, broken arms and stuff, but nothing really too bad."

"Is it hard to get back in there again?"

"Ahh," he smiles. "It takes awhile to get going again," he laughs some more, "but you've gotta get back on. You just have to. I was in a car accident. I got more hurt from that than the bulls. The travelling part is probably more dangerous than riding the bulls. The miles start getting to you after awhile, but I wouldn't trade it for anything."

"What's been the highlight of your career?"

"Going to Calgary . . ."

"That blonde," says Rick Henderson.

Kelly laughs, "Lets not get onto that one . . ."

"Yeah, tell him the whole story," Rick urges him.

"Are the girls more attracted to bull riders than to the other cowboys?"

Bull rider Kelly McEwan prepares for his ride.

"Sometimes . . . we'd like to think so, but I don't think it really matters," Kelly has a slightly smiling, bemused look on his face.

Rick is Kelly's driving partner. "Yeah, we started riding together and travelling together," Rick says.

"I can't get him to drive," Kelly gets in a jab of his own.

"I do his share and everyone else's," Rick replies.

The riders are relaxed. They sit in the shade and discuss life and the bulls. "Who you got?" they ask each other. They want to know which bull the other guy is going to be riding.

They talk about recent rides.

". . . he had you out like this . . ." he leans way over with one arm stretched out straight, "then he turned you right and then he drilled you."

"Yeah," the other rider nods.

"I'm gunner today," Rick says. "I don't like being the first guy out. Some guys like being first, but I don't. I've got Mr. Blue. He's just an average bull, middle of the group. I've talked to other guys who've ridden him."

In a few minutes Rick will be riding. What is he thinking about?

"You really have to concentrate. You have to have positive thoughts and keep at the basics. Don't get thinking about a bad ride. Every day is a new game."

He turns his attention to another bull rider, who asks Rick how he did in Swift Current.

"Got an 85," he replies seriously.

"Yeah," the other guy replies, trying not to show his disappointment. "Good for you."

Rick laughs, "No, I got 73, you're still winning."

The music is turned on full volume and Dave Paulsen is now the man behind the mike, and he has no problem getting the crowd ready for the most dangerous sport in North America.

At Williams Lake they put up additional fencing to make the infield smaller, putting the distance to safety much closer.

I climb up behind the chutes.

Rick rode for the eight seconds but came limping off. "I wasn't impressed with the bull," he says. "On a bull like that you are doing all the work. You can only do what the animal does for you, that's the name of the game."

The judges score both the rider and the bull. Each can get a maximum of 50 points. If the bull doesn't give a good trip, there is only so much the cowboy can do to gain points.

When Kelly McEwan rides, he is off the bull in short order. He stands up and glares at the bull. Stares hard. Stares at him like you would stare at someone who had just beaten you in a bar fight and you want to let him know you'll be back.

"I was just pissed off that he threw me," Kelly tells me. "I was just mad because he beat me. I'll get him next time."

Boyd Patton comes off favoring his arm. "I've got a burner," he explains. "It makes your arm go numb. It's been happening to me all spring."

As I write this he says, "You're writing a book about bull riders? Tell 'em it's a must-see event. One of these days its going to be the biggest sport in the world."

A Leader Among Men

Only cowboys and volunteers are at the Stampede grounds this early in the morning as I wander behind the chutes looking for Earl Call, a stock contractor who owns C+ Rodeo with his brother Roy. A truck is watering down the infield and sprinklers ffsst ffsst ffsst in irregular circles.

I wait to talk to Earl, who is busy, and I watch the cowboys herd the animals into the pens. Earl is directing them where to go. A dog trots along at the feet of the bulls, barking at them, enforcing Earl's orders. "Junior" has excessive confidence for one so small bossing about animals so large and strong. He utilizes speed and moral authority to keep the bulls in line, but the little fellow has a limp and I assume that he's been kicked by a bull. Earl tells me that it is just age catching up with him. Junior has no teeth and suffers from arthritis, but he still does his job as if he was a young pup.

There is still a lot of time before the rodeo is to start and I take up a position in the middle of the picnic table where the riders are gravitating to. The stretching, the going through their ride takes place as usual, but today the guys are more relaxed than any of the previous groups that have come through. If I'd thought about it, which I didn't, I would've thought that by Day Four, and after thousands of miles and three or four other rodeos competed on the weekend, that the guys showing up on the final day would be more road weary, a little more beaten up than the guys that were there on Day One. They're not. I can't detect any difference, except these guys seem more relaxed, in a mood to joke around, and they are more social, talking more with each other individually and in small groups.

This shows their professionalism. They are focused on what they are doing. Life is an adventure, not a lark and they are prepared for the rigors that are required to do their job.

Gerald James is there, so I sit down next to him and ask if he can tell me any special terms that the bull riders use that aren't common to Canadian English. He thinks for a moment, then he says, "Hey Dave, this guy wants to know what terms we use."

The fellow he called walks over and Gerald introduces Dave Leader. He is a solidly built man and looks as if he has just walked off the silver screen, having played the romantic lead in an old style western. In fact he has walked off the silver screen. He lives in Calgary where the movie industry is growing, and has become a stuntman. Recently he got two pages of lines. He's worked on *Sweet Water Redemption* (where he had the speaking part), *Convict Cowboy* and several series such as *Viper*, *Lonesome Dove* and *Honey I Shrunk the Kids*.

To put a Hollywood cowboy actor in the same class as Leader would be an injustice to cowboys. Leader, like most pro riders, is as tough as his boots. I spend an hour with Dave while he dredges up as many words as he can think of. Much of the glossary at the back of this book is Dave's contribution.

He talks and I write. The air is as dry as cowboy humor and the wind whips gritty dust across the page and in my face and eyes and nose and ears.

Dave Leader limps out of the infield after a rough ride at Cereal.

At 32 Dave is getting to be one of the old men in the sport, and after close to 17 years bull riding, all he owns is his pick-up truck. "I don't get any support from my Mom and Dad, like some of the guys do. I used to do 90 to 100 events a year. Now that I'm working in the movies, I'm only doing 30 or 40 rides a year. I am a carpenter by trade, but I've lucked out by getting into the movies."

He has won some 20 buckles, 3 or 4 saddles and numerous "trinkets." His name appears often in the rodeo programs, newspapers and various rodeo publications. He is respected by the other cowboys. He is a likeable guy. He was 19 when he broke into the Professional ranks and had to pay his dues to prove himself with the older riders.

"When you start the attitude towards you is, 'Hey, you little rookie bastard, get in there and drive.' One time I was travelling with some older guys, Bryon Keltts, Tim Thompson and Clayton Hines. I was 19 and they were in their 30s. I'd been driving forever and I was getting real tired," he laughs. "Clayton wakes up and says, 'Hey Leader, if you start getting tired, don't be afraid to pull over and get a coffee.' He didn't offer to drive, or anything. When you're a rookie, they'll give you grief. You're the butt of everyone's jokes."

Not that he hasn't returned the favor when some younger guys have come along. "We filled one guy's rigging bag with rocks. He picked it up as we're rushing to the truck. 'Jesus, this is getting heavy,' he says."

Dave has a way with words and builds images as he describes his experiences. "When you've travelled for miles and miles and hour upon hour, and you're crammed into a car with five sweating, farting, burrito-eating bull riders, you have no illusions about the 'romance' of being on the road. It's hard to say you like the rodeo when you've been travelling 600 miles in a hot stinking car with farting, nose-picking cowboys who haven't showered for days. The young kids don't know how to shave, they don't eat good food, I'd just as soon travel by myself." And now that he's got a steady income, he can afford to. And after the guys read this, he might have to.

There have been changes in the last 20 years. "In the mid-70s it started to change a lot. There are more rodeos now and so many guys just do one event. It used to be that you'd camp in one place and stay for the whole rodeo and get on two head. Now you ride one day and leave. There are more guys riding and the way it is now you might see 3 or 4 guys you saw yesterday but you don't get to know them the way you used to."

And though they may travel for miles and miles, they aren't tourists, "You travel a lot, but you don't really see the country. I've been to Vegas four times but I've never been downtown. You're going down the road at 900 miles an hour (after travelling with the bull riders, I realized this is not much of an exaggeration), you go flying into town, have something to eat, go to the rodeo and then you are off to the next place."

Dave gives me time to write, but he's got lots of stories and people to talk about. "There are some really good guys around. I travelled with J.P. Veitch. He was a stock broker and a lot of the guys didn't want to travel with him. I didn't either at first, I thought he had an attitude and he always talked about money. But we got along really good. He lived in two totally different worlds. He'd spent part of his life wearing a suit and going to an office. On the weekend he'd be going down the road and he was wearing blue jeans and cowboy boots. Once you figured out where he was coming from and what he was all about, he wasn't too bad. I got to like him."

I wipe the page clean of grit. Cowboys sit on the tops of the picnic tables, leaning close to listen to Dave's stories.

"There are some crazy people in this sport," he continues. "One time I was travelling with Dan Lowery and Slew Waters, maybe it was just Slew. We were down in the States driving through the desert. It was about 135 and I was laying in the back seat, just wearing shorts and sweating my ass off. Slew was driving. He was wearing a down filled vest and he's drinking hot coffee from a thermos."

"Tell him . . ." someone interjects and I don't hear exactly what they're talking about. Some stunt they pulled somewhere.

Leader laughs, "We set somebody up with a transvestite. I won't mention any names because he wasn't too amused. We set him up, and the transvestite gives him a blow job. Then, as he's walking away, he pulls his skirt up so that the cowboy could see he's a man. It just about made him sick."

The cowboys laugh. More than one knows this story is true because they were there.

"There are a lot of real cowboys," Leader continues. "There are guys that can go out and chase cattle the way they used to, then get into the arena and be pretty good at the sport. But more and more it is just professional cowboys who are doing this."

"I don't think you'd ever get me back on the broncs," someone says.

"I can't believe that we do what we do for peanuts," Leader continues. "The professional hockey player, football player, baseball player, they're guaranteed a pay cheque whether they sit on the bench or play the entire game. We have no contracts, no guarantees. If we get hurt, we don't get anything."

"You hear about . . ." I didn't get the name of the cowboy, but the story was not an unusual one. "He got hurt and couldn't ride. He had to go to Calgary for therapy and it broke him. He went to the Cowboy Benevolent Fund and he was told that it was only for serious injuries. It's bullshit! What's the Fund there for if it isn't to help guys who need it?"

"And when do they decide it's a serious injury?"

"What may be serious for one guy might not be as big a deal to another guy."

"Yeah, if he's living in Calgary he doesn't have to go somewhere else to get treated. You gotta go into Calgary, pay for someplace to stay, and you're not making any money when you're doing that. It can clean you right out."

"Right now," says Clint Ellis, "I have a lawsuit with the CPRA (Canadian Pro Rodeo Association). I can't rodeo here. Our right to work is limited by them. I should be able to rodeo where I want. Cowboys live out of a suitcase and things haven't improved for them. Ponoka has the same payout today as they did in 1984. They can do that because they know we'll come. I won here last year, but this year I can't ride because of this bullshit."

They all talk at once. There are a number of stories of disgruntled cowboys. Disgruntled with the CPRA.

"The Association is trying to control it too much," Dave says. "It is not an Association for the cowboy anymore. It is suppose to help us, but it's hurting us. It's keeping us from where we want to go. We've formed our own association, the CBR, the Canadian Bull Riders association. You should talk to Wes Cyr. We're holding our own bull ridings and all the profits come back to the cowboys and don't go to some promoter."

This subject was to come up several times.

But there are other things on Dave's mind. He admits that a lot of the stories about "bad drinking guys" are true. Having fun can mean just about anything. "We were just in Olds (Alberta) where we got into a big bar clearing brawl," he looks down while he talks. "A lot of people think cowboys are rough, dirty people. They got that image from the '60s, and it's a bad rap. How many professional sports people have drug problems? You won't find that in rodeo. They'll drink beer and whiskey, but they're not into drugs. I'm 32 now, so I've got to take care of myself. I go to the gym and work out. Most of the guys are pretty clean living."

Bernie Bowe leans over and says, "I'm 37 now. You gotta stay in shape or you can't rodeo. You can't be drinking every night or you're not going to be able to get up the next morning and ride. You don't ride well if you're bent out of shape."

"Hey Leader," Derek Adams calls across to him, "I hear you beat a couple of guys up in Olds when it went western."

"No, I didn't," Dave replies.

"I heard you were right into it."

"Yeah, I was right in the middle of it. But I only beat up one guy. I beat up the same guy up twice."

Everyone laughs.

"I knew I could beat him up, so why should I pick on someone else I didn't know if I could beat?"

Then he explains to me, "We were having a drink in the bar there and this guy started giving me a bad time. Sometimes the townies like to prove how tough they are. I wasn't interested in fighting with this guy, but he wouldn't leave me alone, so we got into it. Then his friends got into it, and my friends and the bouncers and it turned into a good old fashioned bar clearing fight. I wish a few more guys had been there."

But now it is time to ride bulls and they disperse to get ready. They get into their heads, or do whatever they need to, to prepare for their ride.

During the bull riding there is the usual exuberance and disappointment. One rider has a good ride and he struts to the fence, hands in the air, index fingers thrusting alternatively into the air. A very rare display of emotion. Derek Adams rides his bull close to the eight seconds, and it is a call the judges have to make to whether he stayed on long enough. They say he wasn't. "How long do you have to ride them for here?" he snipes as he climbs the fence. "Fifteen seconds!?"

The winners are decided on the final day, but the paycheques are mailed out so the cowboy won't see his money from this Cowboy Christmas for some time yet. If he's earned any. More than 40 of the cowboys who have made the trip to Williams Lake won't get a penny for their efforts.

A Wise Guy

At the end of Day Three of the Williams Lake Stampede I was standing by the rodeo office behind the chutes when I noticed a cowboy lingering nearby. He wasn't a competitor, as he had an old camera slung around his neck and I'd seen him taking pictures during the events. He was wearing a beat up black cowboy hat, and has a moustache gone mostly white with streaks of black. His face is lined and scarred and there is an intensity in his voice that reverberates in his eyes and attitude.

"Who you shooting for?" he's a bit aggressive in his attitude.

I keep writing and don't look up from the page. "Myself."

"You with a newspaper?"

"No," I continue to write.

"Where you from?"

"I'm doing a book about the bull riders."

"Yeah?"

I can sense his skepticism. He is giving me the attitude that I'm in his backyard and I'd better prove I have the right to be there. I'm not interested in proving myself, but I start asking him questions, and get a lot more information than I could have anticipated. This is Don Wise, a fellow who turns out to be very interesting, knowledgeable and helpful.

Don has extensive rodeo experience, most of it riding bareback and in the Wild Horse race, which has got to be one of the crazier events in the rodeo. Three guys grab a bucking horse, put a saddle on it, and one rides it across the finish line. Getting that wild horse in a mood to be ridden is no easy task. Probably about the same process as it was to get Don to settle down. But now with a wife and a precocious daughter he is about as settled as he can be.

Don and his wife Miriam produce the magazine *Wolf Howls*, for the Tsilhqot'in Nation. Don is a celebrity. His readers respect him for his passionate writing that is reflected in the headline of his column 'Wolf Howls at the Moon.' In the May issue the headline states, "The simple, right word has power and passion."

Don Wise, a former rodeo competitor who loves every aspect of the sport.

"Who've you written for?" he wants to know.

"Canadian Press, the four daily newspapers in Japan, the *Mail* on Sunday, Newsday, the daily papers in Cyprus and Malta, the *Vancouver Sun*, more magazines than I care to mention and I owned and edited a weekly newspaper for seven years."

He takes a step back, "So you've paid your dues."

I didn't look up from my writing. "You wanna go for a beer?" I ask.

"Okay," he relents. He doesn't normally hang around the beer gardens.

We go up to the beer gardens – which is obviously a place where they grow beer, because it certainly had no relationship with flowers. Once there, however, Don was quickly monopolized by other people, so I bid him adieu and said I would see him tomorrow.

Throughout most of the following day I didn't see Don and thought that he was going to renege on his offer of giving me his book. But when the bull riding started he was there and afterwards we went over to his camper, where I met Miriam and their energetic and delightful daughter, Jessee.

"When you are talking to a cowboy ask him about his buckle," Don advises. "A buckle shows that a cowboy has paid his dues. It is part of the lore of the rodeo. When you are looking at the rodeo cowboy, you are looking at his buckle. It is the highwater mark of his career so far."

This was an excellent piece of advice and, from then on, when I saw someone dressed like a cowboy I checked out his buckle, because that was the one piece of hardware that could not be copied. A man might wear a beaten cowboy hat, Wrangler jeans and cowboy boots and still not be a rodeo competitor. If the man was wearing a rodeo buckle he wasn't a drug store cowboy.

Don agrees that the Williams Lake Stampede has a real mystique about it. The top cowboys love to compete here, making it one of the harder places to win. "I first entered here in 1965," Don says, "and I didn't win here 'til 1990. I won a buckle, which is something I will pass on to my daughter."

Don talked extensively about Calgary, giving me names of people to talk to and places to go. He strongly urged me to contact Calgary right away for a press pass. "Right now!" he snapped at me. "If you don't, when you get to Calgary you'll run into a wall. A wall that you won't get around."

He was right. I had a hard time getting over it too.

On the back of *Chute that Horse* are two pictures of Don. His intense brown eyes stare up at the camera, exactly the same way as in the picture I took of him two decades later. The moustache was blacker then, and the face less scarred. The other picture of him is at the Williams Lake Stampede, July 1, 1965 on the back of Paper Doll. Paper Doll was anything but a paper doll, giving Don a neck injury that kept him out of rodeo for ten years.

Chute that Horse was the 1976 winner of the Interior Rodeo Association's Bert Roberts Memorial Award – given annually to the person who has contributed the most to the promotion of the sport of rodeo. Don continues to promote the rodeo based on an understanding that few other sports writers have.

Good thing I didn't tell him to piss off when he stuck his nose in my notebook and demanded to know what I was doing, and wanting to know if I had paid my dues. It was the beginning of a friendship that I hope will continue for some time.

Chute that Horse is a photo book that contains some great stories. During a quiet moment on the ferry back to Vancouver Island, I perused it and enjoyed reading "A bull riding classic," which is one of the best descriptions I've ever read about the process of getting on and off a bull. With Don's kind permission I reprint it here:

DIGHTMAN vs. HEAD HUNTER

It's mighty rare when a cowboy turns down a drink with his partners at stampede time. Mertis Dightman did it once. It was just after he drew the rankest bull that ever did make it to the Williams Lake Stampede. That was in 1970 when Mertis dropped in to the Lakeview beer parlor to see who was entered up in the bull riding.

That tough decision signaled the determination and resolve that everybody at the beer table knew would produce a bull riding classic.

Nobody was disappointed.

Dightman, a big, powerful, black bull rider had just flown in from Texas for a shot at the big bull riding purse. But the draw was crucial.

It would take the best ride from the RCA circuit's best rider – on the best bull – to win.

Mertis drew it. At the time, Head Hunter was the bull that drew beads of cold sweat on every cowboy's forehead. With good reason.

Head Hunter got his name from his favorite quirk of slamming his horns into any cowboy's head who made the mistake of putting it in range after getting out of shape as the bull cranked it up in front of the chutes.

He got a few too. So to ease the smart a bit, the points of the horns were cut off. But just the points.

There was plenty left to gore a man if he got hung up in his bull rope after being bucked off.

And, to heighten the drama, the Brahma-Mexican fighting bull cross had never been ridden.

Dightman knew all this. The rawhide telegraph filled him in on Head Hunter's recent escapades.

So, although it was only eight o'clock, Mertis checked into a motel and went to bed. He said he figured he might have a few seconds hard work to do tomorrow afternoon.

He was right. But the eight seconds that Mertis was on Head Hunter's back were not much more intense than the four hours he took psyching himself up for the grim confrontation.

He spent most of that time alone. He was getting his rope ready. Right up until he gingerly snuck the braided rope under Head Hunter's belly, Mertis was meticulously examining it for flaws, buffing it up with a wire brush, and smoking rosin into the hand hold loop and his leather riding glove.

As the bull riding event got closer, the many cowboys hanging around the chute area started to dig their thumbs a little deeper into their jean pockets and kick a little harder at the lumps of dirt in front of the chute gates.

And their eyes started to shoot anxious glances at chute number four.

Announcer Bud Stewart was haranguing the crowd about Head Hunter's infamy.

The bull was fouling Mertis in the chute. His grisly body was slamming the sides of the chute and his lethal head was snaking back at Dightman as he wrapped up his hand, settling down close to the bull's humped back.

Mertis couldn't get in position – clamped tight against his rope with his long shanked spurs pointed straight into the bull's belly.

When the bull felt the tingle of steel he reared back smashing his head into Mertis's face, stunning him and bloodying his nose. To get his bull out of the chute, Mertis would have to give the gateman a nod then drop into position as the bull reared from the hated cage just as the chute gate flew open.

He did just that, and got out into the arena in good position despite a frantic lunge and high spinning buck out of the chute on the first jump.

For seven and a half seconds Dightman brought the crowd to its feet with the most exciting man-beast showdown they had ever seen.

Dightman clung up tight against his riggin' and managed to bang plenty of iron into the bull's belly.

Then that hump flashed up and onto Mertis's free hand – just enough to force judge Lawrence Lamb to technically disqualify the rider.

But Mertis hung on for eight seconds and wrote himself into the unofficial folklore of pro rodeo – if not the score sheets.

Bruce Watt, who was on hand for the ride, said if Mertis had not been goose-egged he could have written his own score.

But Dightman's trouble was not over at the whistle. There was still the matter of getting off the bull's back.

With the help of a blinding action from the clown's coat, Mertis sprawled over the bull. He managed to free his hand from its rosin clutch and was thrown free of Head Hunter's fury.

As Mertis walked dejected back to the chutes winding up his bull rope, the crowd erupted in a frenzy and many surged forward to shake the hand of the man who had just given them the biggest sporting thrill of their lives.

The first man to grab his hand was stock contractor Dave Perry.

And as Dightman wiped the caked blood off his smashed face and leaned back to quench his parched throat with a cold beer, the usually staid cowboys were already laying the groundwork for a piece of hardcore rodeo folklore.

Calgary is the Big Show. It is the cowboy's Stanley Cup, World Series, Christmas and Easter all rolled into one.

Jack Daines

Calgary sucks!

the sentiment of some bull riders

The Big Show

Wednesday morning, before doing anything else (Don Wise's admonitions still ringing in my ears) I sent a fax to Brian Ratcliffe, who is in charge of the media for the Calgary Stampede, requesting accreditation. Much to my surprise he phoned me back late in the evening, one hour later. He told me bluntly that he couldn't give me a media pass as there was no space left.

I accepted this as it was only hours before the 1997 edition of the Calgary Exhibition and Stampede was to get underway. It was a little late for me to be applying. I spent a lot of those hours traveling from Victoria to Calgary.

I take the C-Train to the Stampede the next morning. I stand next to a cowboy and as we get close to the grounds I ask him what events he's in.

"I'm up here for the Police and Fire Games," he tells me in a soft southern drawl. "I rode in the saddle bronc and the bull riding."

"How did you do?"

"I won the bull riding," Danny Booth says with no overblown sense of pride. He only told me because I asked. Danny, a police officer with the Oklahoma City Police, was a very sincere individual with a lot to say.

While we were entering the grounds we were given an "Opening Day Commemorative PIN" in a small plastic bag stapled to a card with "UP CLOSE RODEO" printed in large letters. The Calgary Stampede arena is enormous, especially in comparison to all the other Canadian rodeos I've seen, and unfortunately for most of the thousands of people in the stands, they are a long way from the action. It is not like the smaller rodeos where you can smell and hear the animals as they use their brute strength in their battle with the cowboy. But there is a lot of entertainment. It's a bigger show all round.

I am a little disappointed with the first day's bull riding. The stock is too good, and too in control. They all dispose of their riders in short order then trot off to the chutes. There aren't any that want to showboat. There are no real rank bulls that want to take a tear at someone, anyone. It is as if they were told to be on their best behavior.

Danny, who is now 38, started riding when he was 21 and just out of the U.S. Marines. A late start for the professional bull rider.

"On my first ride," he says with a slight smile, "it was in Blanchard. I rode for a 70 or so, then I got hung up. I rode that bull longer after the horn than before it." He chuckles.

"What do you think when you're out there?" I ask.

"I really don't think," he replies. "I just do what I've got to do. I try to not outguess the bull."

Danny is waiting for his friend Terry West to ride. Terry is also from Henryetta, Oklahoma. Danny has great respect for West's bull riding abilities. He is the only one to have ridden the rank Bodacious twice. The same Bodacious that mashed Tuff Hedeman's face.

"He's got tremendous talent," says Danny of West. "He's an aggressive rider. He's really focussed."

Bull rider Danny Booth at the Calgary Stampede.

"What is an aggressive rider?"

"An aggressive rider is one who uses his feet well. You don't let the bull get to you. If you are going to ride the real rank ones you've really got to ride them, not just get on them."

Danny has won lots of trophies and saddles. "I used to go to about 10 rodeos a month," he explains. "Now I go to about 25 or 30 a year. I'm riding as well as I used to, but it is the travelling that gets to you. You don't like being away all the time. And you get tired of always being sore."

"Are there any differences between saddle bronc riding and bull riding?"

"They are both hard, but for different reasons," he answers. He ignores the guy who goes by selling beer. Sitting in the hot sun, frying my uncovered head, I wouldn't mind having a beer, but it's difficult to write and drink at the same time. "Saddle Bronc riding is timing and finesse. You get into the rhythm of the horse. With the bulls you need strength, co-ordination and balance. The bull is throwing a lot of weight so you need strength to stay on your rope, but strength is only one factor. A big guy is not going to ride any better than a smaller man. The biggest part of bull riding is mental."

Danny went to a bull riding school where he learned the basics, learning about the equipment, learning the proper ways to get on a bull, and learning to do certain things right. "Professionals critique what you are doing, and that helps a lot."

Advice from other riders is always available, but not always useful.

"Everybody offers help," Danny says. "Probably half of them don't know what they are talking about. When you're not riding well you've got 15 guys telling you what to do, and then you look at what they are doing and they're not riding any better than you are.

"What you've got to do is watch the guys on top. Something got them there. I used to watch Lane Frost, Cody Custer and Tuff Hedeman. Jim Sharp is an excellent guy to watch."

"What made Frost good?"

"He always seemed to be in control of his ride. Everybody has an individual style and though everyone has to do the basics well, there are variables such as the size and the build of the rider and who taught him to ride."

Danny explains why he, and most cowboys, doesn't like to be the gunner. "I like being down the line a bit," he states. "It gives you a bit more time to prepare. The judges are likely to score the first guy a little bit lower because they don't know what's coming. They have to have some room to move up. Unless the guy gives a really great ride."

We watch with interest as the bull riding continues and J.W. Hart scores the highest ride of the day.

"I never complain about my score," Danny continues. "I'm not always happy with it, but usually it is myself I'm unhappy with because I didn't do something well. I'm not happy with my ride, not the judges."

"Do you ever get afraid out there?"

"You feel a bit of fear, but it is not something you think about. If there wasn't any fear you should probably quit. I've been afraid, but I've never turned out a bull because I was afraid of it. Some of my best rides have been on bulls I was afraid of, thinking there was no way I could do this bull. I like the bulls. They've got personality. I've got a lot of respect for a good bull."

When Jim Leatherberry rides (and does no better than he did in Williams Lake) Danny likens him to Gordie Howe, for his longevity in the sport.

"You ever been embarrassed out there?" It wasn't Leatherberry's ride that sparked this question.

"Yeah," Danny smiles. "I was riding at . . . Jackpot." Because of the noise of the crowd I couldn't hear the name of where this ride took place.

"The bull I had was not a good bull and I rode him to the horn then I jumped off and landed on my feet, but I landed squatted down. I stood up and walked off to the fence where I started cleaning my rope. I heard some laughter from some girls in the bleachers behind me, but I didn't know what they were laughing at, so I paid it no attention and went on cleaning my rope.

"A friend came over and asked me what happened. 'Nothing happened,' I replied. 'I did my ride and I stepped off.'"

"'You're bleeding.'

"I thought he was razzing me. 'Yeah sure,' I said.

"'You wearing red underwear?'

"'No.'

"I was still standing in front of those girls," he goes through the motions of cleaning the rope. "Yeah, they were laughing at me, and I had no idea what they were laughing at until I noticed I had a big rip in the seat of my jeans. When I had landed I came down on my rawl and it ripped my pants. I still have a scar on one cheek."

When the day's riding is finished we shake hands, and Danny disappears into the crowd.

The Next Lane Frost

The next day, I finally get a chance to talk to Brian Ratcliffe. I explain to him that I want interviews with an announcer, a rodeo clown and one or two stock contractors, and ask him again if it is possible to get a pass.

No, he couldn't do it. But he could arrange the interviews.

"How many media are there at the Stampede?" I ask.

"2200."

"What is the furthest away they are from?"

"South Africa."

"Phone over to the rodeo office and ask them to set up those interviews," he instructs the receptionist.

I thank him for his help, and wait while the call is made.

"If you go right away talk to Ron Swagger. He'll help you," the secretary tells me.

I walk quickly through the grounds, and pass two men talking outside the rodeo office. I walk into the media trailer and I'm told that Ron is one of the two men outside.

He is the one with the gray beard, and a different attitude than Ratcliffe's. He's very helpful. He takes me into the office and gives me a lot of material on the rodeo that turns out to be invaluable. I reiterate what I want to do.

"Bill Kehler, the announcer, has an office out here. You can get him after today's events. I'll have to set up an interview with Keith Isley and I'll see if I can get a stock contractor to talk to you. You'll have to wait here."

"Any chance of going in?" I ask as we walk outside.

"If Brian didn't give you a pass there is nothing I can do," Ron replies, and he gets in his golf cart and drives off.

I don't know why but I'm about as pissed off as I can be. I don't get upset at a hell of a lot, but for some reason this annoys the shit out of me. "Well, I'll just do it my own way!" I sit down on the steps and start to read the media guide Ron gave me.

Suddenly the golf cart reappears from around the corner and Ron stops in front of me. "I can give you a day pass," he says. He goes into the office and returns in a moment with a green slip, which he gives me.

I hop into the cart. We go through an underground passage under the race track and into the area behind the infield. I'm elated. I know this is where I am going to get the best stories.

The stock contractors are sitting at the tables in the beer garden and I talk with Wayne Vold and Bruce Sunstrum, two men with very different natures. When they leave to watch the bull riding I go to the railing around the infield and sit on the top rail. I have one of the best seats in the house. I look up at the grandstands that are teaming with fans, and when they roar, as they do when Isley runs around the field holding on to the saddle of his horse that is galloping at a good clip, the sound comes flooding down.

Sitting on the rail are two girls chatting about the cowboys. "Poster Boy is up first," one says to the other.

Isley is on stage doing his act. He is bent over in "pain."

"What's the matter?" the announcer asks in his deep baritone voice.

"My knee is locked," the clown whines in great distress.

"Your knee?"

"Yes," he flexes a leg. "It's not my right knee."

"You're right knee is okay."

"It's not my left knee."

"Well, if it's not your right knee and it's not your left knee, what is it?"

"It's my high knee."

"Keith!"

"I've broken it."

"You've broken it?"

"Yeah, there's a crack in it."

The announcer laughs along with the audience.

"But it goes this way," he moans plaintively. "It's a good thing it didn't go the other way because then when I went down a slide it would go blublbublblub," he vibrates his libs over his finger.

"You know one of the riders?" I ask the girl next to me. She's wearing a black halter top, displaying a lot of midrift, and tight jeans.

"Robert Bowers," she says.

They are Tracy and Tammy and it is Tammy that is "friends" with Robert. "I've known him for about three years," she says. "But we're just friends. That's all. Just friends."

She goes away for a while. Tracy says she knows some of the riders, but she's not dating any of them.

I ask if she worries about them when they ride.

"No. I don't get too worried. They know what they are doing, and it is not all that dangerous. Tammy worries a lot."

When Tammy returns she concurs with Tracy. "It scares the shit out of me."

"WE WILL, WE WILL, ROCK YOU!" The music is pumped up, the announcer tries to get the crowd into it, but the distances here are great, and it is hard to tell if people are really into it.

Again the stock is good and the riders are biting the dust in quick order.

"There is only one way off . . ." the announcer says as a cowboy is flung from the bull. "You better keep all your ducks in a row or he'll deposit you in the outhouse."

There are some good rides, and everyone gets away cleanly. No serious wrecks today.

Robert Bowers rides over when the event is finished and he chats quietly with Tammy for a moment. He has a long scar underneath his chin which Tammy later tells me about.

"Robert was in the worst wreck in Calgary last year," she says.

"How bad was it?"

"He was hung up for a long time. I don't know exactly how long, but they have eight pictures of him," she says. "That's how long he was in that wreck. But it got him in the stats. He got stepped on and broke his jaw in 9 places. Then he went out and placed second in Rodeo Royal. The doctors told him not to ride, but he did. He's very tough."

We walk towards the beer gardens.

"He doesn't drink and he doesn't smoke either," she adds. "He's the next Lane Frost."

"You going to get married?"

"No!" she shouts in response to my question. "We're not going together. We're just friends! Bull riders can't have steady girlfriends. It just doesn't work. They are always on the road and girlfriends only get in the way." She seems clear about this. "He wants to rodeo for a while, and after that he might settle down," her black cowboy hat shades her eyes. "But I didn't say with whoever." She makes it absolutely clear that they are not a number. "He travels alone a lot. That way he doesn't have to worry about another person."

Tracy has been listening. "There are a lot of stories about the cowboys and how rough they are," she interjects. "But the ones who are serious about the sport don't drink a lot and they don't do drugs. About all they do is chew tobacco. They have a job to do and they work very hard at it. People don't realize how hard a sport it is."

People are walking by and I'm looking for Ron Swagger, but I don't see him.

"There is a bull-o-rama in Strathmore at 6:30. They finish up here and they go straight there. Then they'll drive to Oregon where they'll ride on Sunday and be back in Calgary Monday to ride slack Tuesday morning. You can't do that kind of schedule if you are in the bar all night."

That doesn't mean they don't get to the bar, or they don't drink.

"Hi, Dave, how you doing," I shake hands with Dave Leader, who's just coming into the beer garden.

"Floyd, you made it," his big hand engulfs mine. "Hey, there's a bull-o-rama out at Strathmore at 6:30. You want to go?"

"Sure."

"I'm not going, but I'll see if I can get you someone to ride with," he looks around. "Clint, you're going to Strathmore, can you give this guy a lift?" He starts to introduce me.

"Yeah, sure, we met in Williams Lake." Clint Ostrem shakes hands.

"This is Jay Manning," Dave introduces him.

"Yeah, we met in Victoria," I said shaking his hand.

Jay smiles broadly. "Yes, I remember." He always seems to be smiling. His face still has that youthful enthusiasm I had noticed at Luxton. He hasn't had a chance to stop and rest like I've had. He should have been dead tired, but like the rest of the riders, he's traveling on an energy most of us don't possess.

"You sure you got room for me?" I totally forget about meeting Keith Isley.

"Yeah, sure, no problem," they both say. "This is Shelly Jones," Jay's girlfriend. She's a robust looking young lady with a lot of spirit. We walk quickly towards the parking lot. There's a sense of urgency. Everyone would like to hang out at the beer gardens and have a beer but there is no time for that now. They've got to get on the road.

The cowboy has to be able to travel. It wears you down. There are cowboys who can ride 40 miles from home, but when they start traveling they're toast.

Jack Johansen
Former Bull Rider and
Bull Riding Instructor

Tuffanuff

Jay slings his rigging bag over his shoulder and limps across the parking lot towards his car.

"You okay?" I ask.

"I got stepped on in Ponoka last week. It was just getting healed up and I got stepped on again last night. I got slammed down real good," he gives me a smile over his shoulder.

Clint has a truck and he drives it to the Crossroads Motor Inn where he parks it. "A lot of the cowboys leave their vehicles there. They keep an eye on them for us," he explains.

We go to a nearby gas station to fill up. We rush into the convenience store where I buy a thick sandwich and a bottle of juice. It's the first thing I've eaten since breakfast. Everybody grabs something to eat and we rush back to the car. It is already six o'clock and we are still a long way from Strathmore.

I get in the back seat of the car and listen and write, eat my sandwich and drink the juice.

"I got more cowboy in the end of my dink than he does in his whole body," Clint is saying to Jay. I didn't hear the whole story, but someone was unhappy with his travelling partner.

Shelly sits in the front with Jay and I ask her what she does.

"I'm a barrel racer," she answers.

I laugh, then explain that I'm not laughing at her. "I could've almost told you that. Every bull rider I've met that is married is married to a barrel racer."

"We're not married yet."

"You've got to have the same sense . . . the same interests," she says, then she asks me where I'm from.

"Williams Lake."

"Me too!"

Being from Williams Lake is a good thing in the rodeo world and it is the first time that I ever felt that being from there did me any good.

"I live in Victoria now," I add, then ask if she is good at her event.

"No," she responds bluntly and we laugh.

"How long you been riding?"

"A long time."

We roll along 16th Avenue, caught up in traffic, anxious to get on the open highway.

Clint explains that the bull-o-rama is put on by the bull riders themselves. They have formed a bull riding co-op and all the riders are shareholders. "It started two years ago. There are no entry fees and the prize money is higher. So the contestants get more of the money rather than it going to some promoter. We expect to get dividends from it at some point."

The bull riders like the bull-o-ramas, where theirs is the only event. They don't have to waste a lot of time waiting around for other events to take place, and they have a better payday. They are the uncontested stars of the show.

"I guess winning the Canadian Championship helped you a lot," I say to Jay.

Jay has an unfortunate habit of liking to look at the person he's talking to. Unfortunate when you're in the back seat and he's driving and he's got the pedal to the metal. "Yeah," he says over his shoulder. "Just after Ponoka it started working. Then I got the money and I could play a bit more and not always be worrying about the next rodeo."

I'm balancing my drink between my knees, writing and trying to watch the road for him.

On the highway, outside the city limits, the cars pass quickly behind us, and slow traffic in the fast lane moves out of our way when we come flying up behind them. It is not for the thrill he's driving fast. It is like it is the cowboy's right to drive fast. They are going down the road, and that's how its done –*fast*.

We get talking about travelling and different living conditions and Clint, with his characteristic good humor and quirky mischievous smile, has a story to tell. "A couple of years ago I stayed at Al Soul's for a month. He put up a lot of the cowboys. His was the place you went when you were in Calgary and you didn't have anywhere to go.

"The first day I'm there I decide I need a shower and I guess I didn't get the shower curtain quite closed, because when I'm finished there is water all over the place. I mopped it up, and I thought I'd done a pretty good job of it, but it's not good enough for Al. He comes and gets me from my room and takes me into the shower and he tells me how to shower and how to clean up afterwards and he belittles me. He embarrasses me in front of the other guys. I'm really pissed off at this. You know he could've said something, but he didn't have to embarrass me in front of the other guys.

"So about an hour later he jumps in the shower and while he's in there I get a squeeze ball and I squirt water under the doorway.

"Al gets out of the shower and he sees the floor is soaked, so he comes out and says to me, 'Geez Clint, I guess I've got to apologize to you. I guess the tub is leaking. I'm going to have to fix it.'

"I kept that secret from him for about two years until I told Derek Martineou and it got back to Al. He didn't talk to me for a week."

"Soon as you tell one guy," Jays says, "it's going to get back to him."

"Yeah, I shouldn't have told anyone, especially not Derek."

The Olds we're riding in is Jay's mother's. "Where's your truck?" Clint asks.

"It broke down in Colorado Springs," Jay says looking over his shoulder.

"The tow truck driver pulled out the tranie," Shelly adds. "It's going to cost us $3500 to get it fixed."

"That's why I don't drive anything I can't tip over in the ditch," Clint says.

"You are going back to Calgary?" I think to ask.

Jay smiles at me, "Don't worry, if we don't get you back, there's sure to be someone who's going."

The Olds whips up a cloud of dust as we tear through the parking lot and right up to the back gate behind the Strathmore grounds. Jay wants to drive right in where the stock and the vehicles that brought them are parked.

The lady at the gate comes up to the window and leans in, "You can't go in there, Jay. Why don't you just park it alongside there? You'd better hurry up, they're getting ready to start. Hi Clint. You got two guests."

Jay parks the car and we all hop out on the run. Jay and Clint grab their bags and Jay limps off as quickly as he can with the bad leg, and he's doing a good clip for being so banged up.

"Hey, wait, you gotta get stamped," the gate lady calls to us. We stop and get our hands stamped and continue on. We go through another check point and the young man there doesn't know that this is Jay Manning the

Canadian Champion, and Clint Ostrem, bull rider supreme, and he tries to stop them to check to see if they're stamped, but he gets ignored for his trouble. Shelly keeps going too, but I assure him that they're all stamped and he takes my word for it.

And we can hear announcer Pete Montana welcoming the fans who are still filing in and about half filling the stands.

Jay and Clint join the two dozen or so bull riders behind the chutes where they're changing their clothes. Shelly and I climb a fence, jump down on the other side and send up puffs of dust as we hit ground. We go to the small stands across the infield from the grandstand. We've got a view behind the chutes and of the arena, so it's a pretty good place to sit.

Shelly takes the list of the evening's riders and keeps track of the scores.

"Why do you do that?" I ask. "Do you keep track of how well Jay does?"

"No, it just gives me something to do. It can be boring in the stands by yourself."

The crowd is not bored this evening, as there is some fine stock and some pretty decent riding. Jordie Campbell gets an 83 and struts off.

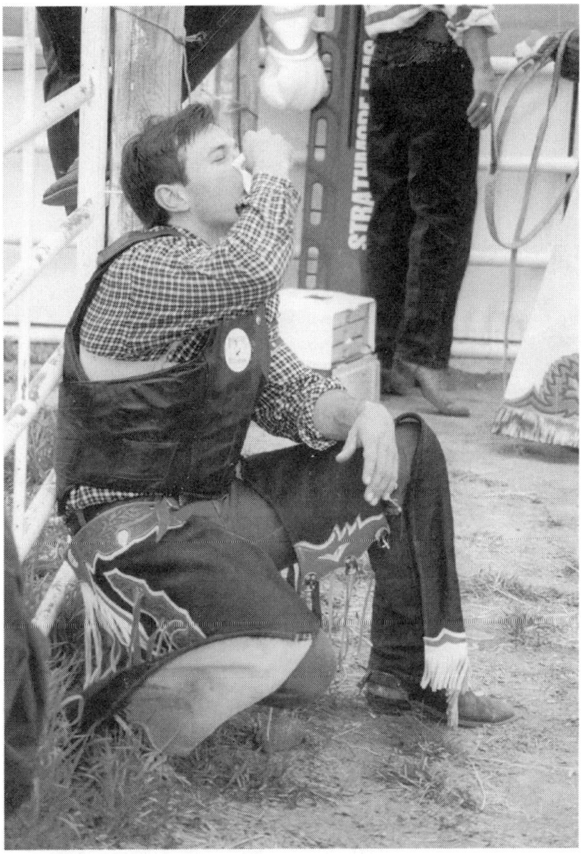

"Has he got an attitude?" Shelly asks.

I demonstrated his actions after his ride in Williams Lake. Jabbing his fingers at the sky.

"He does have an attitude," she responds.

Jason Matlock comes off and as he's walking to the fence, he's digging into his mouth for his chaw of tobacco, which he flings out. He spits what his fingers didn't get. His head goes down. He got head butted and his nose is bleeding seriously. The first aid attendants have a look at him and he sits on the ground with his head back against the rails. Sits there for a long time. When we see him later he's fine and doesn't seem at all bothered by the job done on his nose.

"You get nervous when Jay rides?" I ask.

"No. Yeah, I do," she displays fingers with the nails gnawed down.

"What's he doing?" Shelly draws my attention to Jay, who is behind the chutes, moving around. "He did a full turn. What an idiot!" she exclaims. "He's dancing! It looks kind of cute, actually. Look at him!"

She gets more agitated as his turn to ride approaches and both Clint and Jay draw mediocre bulls and both score 75s. They are tied for 9th and 10th positions. The final money positions, and the ones that get a chance to ride in the second round for the big money.

There are four riders left to go, and we hold our breath hoping that they won't score. The first one is Bucked Off. Shelly marks BO beside his name. The second one bites the dust, then the third and finally the last one gets bucked and Jay and Clint are in the finals.

"Damn, I thought we were going to get home soon," Shelly says. But she is not as surprised as Jay is. While we are waiting for the second half to get underway, Shelly talks with Jay. She comes back laughing. "What a pea brain," she says. "He was all untaped, had his pants off and was ready to go home and I told him he has to ride again. He didn't believe me. He had to go up to the booth to check."

To add to the drama, the 10 top riders draw the bulls that they will ride in the final. The bulls are top notch and only three riders stick. Jeff Whitlow goes the 8 seconds and rides to a 90 mark, winning the jackpot. Both Clint and Jay are bucked off.

The bull riders are happy to take a little time to sign hats, t-shirts or whatever the fans want autographed.

I find some time on my hands, as the guys are required to sign autographs, and the line-up for signatures and a chance to have a word with the bull riders is long.

I read the program which has an explanation of the Canadian Professional Bullriders Co-operative Ltd., written by its president, Wes Cyr. In part it reads:

. . . we are a self based group of Canadian bull riders who had the insight two years ago to create a bull riding association for Canada's elite bull riders.

With the danger involved in our exciting sport . . . it has been a great sell to the many fans at rodeos across our nation, we decided to put together some bull ridings to further enhance your enjoyment. We feel by offering you an action packed performance of the best bull riders and the rankest bulls in Canada, our sport will do nothing but flourish for all the betterment of the industry.

The C.P.B. has only the best of the best bull riders, including such bull riders as 1996 Canadian champion Jay Manning, 1995 Canadian champion Wes Cyr, 1993-1994 Canadian champion Wayde Joyal, and 1989 Canadian champion Glen Keeley, as well as all of Canada's other top bull riders.

It's time bull riders were recognized for their athletic ability – after all, we are athletes just like in any other sport! It takes a very special individual to be willing to put it all on the line for eight seconds. With the physical impact a 2000 pound bull has on a 150 pound body, the longevity of the bull riders' careers are shorter than that of any other rodeo event. With bull riding events standing on their own with larger paydays, it will lengthen the bull rider's careers.

This also greatly enhances the corporate sponsors' exposure that they need to receive. By having bull riders in one place for more than a couple of hours, it gives the sponsor the opportunity to become involved on an individual level by marketing their products through retail appearances. This will expose the bull riders' names like other athletes, thus increasing awareness of the products they are endorsing.

The lack of recognition for what they do is something that irks the cowboys, their families and their fans. This lack of recognition would occasionally be brought up, but it wasn't harped upon. There was very little the cowboy did harp about.

A lack of recognition isn't a problem this Saturday evening in Strathmore, as the fans wait patiently for t-shirts, hats, programs and other memorabilia to be signed. The cowboys sit at a long table, laughing and joking with each other and with the fans. They all stay until the last request for a signature or a photo has been made. Jason Matlock is in there with them, showing no signs of the head butting he'd taken an hour earlier. He looked as if he had been in a good deal of pain.

I ask a young lady if she likes the bull riding. She's wearing a t-shirt which across her chest says "Hey Wussy Boy" and on the back, "TUFFANUFF."

"Yeah," she says.

"Why?"

"It's neat."

"Why?"

"It's exciting."

"Scary?"

"No."

"Would you ride a bull?"

"Yeah," she says as she starts to walk away. "I'm going to be the first girl bull rider."

The next Lane Frost no doubt.

The Johansen Brothers

"We're heading over to the hospitality tent," Jay says when the autograph signing is finished. He limps off around the field where the hospitality tent is set up.

We go into the tent and there's some food and Coors Lights. I get a beer.

"You had a pretty good crowd out there tonight," I say to the cowboy standing next to me.

"We had about 2500," he responds, obviously pleased with that number.

"What do you do?"

"Tonight I was stripping the chute," Ray Corkum replies.

"What's that?"

"When the bulls come out of the arena, you gotta make sure the flank is off them. The flank is a rope that goes around their hind quarters and it makes them kick out more with their hind feet so they don't crow hop."

"Sounds like a tough job."

"No, it's got a quick release on it. It's not hard work."

I ask him about his background and tells me that he's from Nova Scotia.

"I rode for about five years," Ray says, "mostly in Texas. I went to school there. My career ended when I tore my knee all to pieces. I caught it on a gate coming out of the chute. In this sport you get hurt a lot of times, but the right one finishes you."

The wrong one might do it too, I think.

"Really, if you are writing a book about bull riding, you should talk to Jack," he says. "He can tell you a lot more about the sport than I can."

He takes me over to where Jack is standing, and I say hello and tell him what I'm doing. He says his name is Jack and he used to ride bulls, but now he's working in town.

"What's your last name?"

"Johansen," he says.

My jaw drops.

"Really! Gees I'm really pleased to meet you. You guys are legends!"

He doesn't seem bothered by my excitement at meeting him, nor at my reiterating the praise that I've heard about him and his four brothers.

Over 25 years the Johansen brothers were a dominant force in Canadian bull riding. In 1972 Jack went to the National High School Finals in Denver and in 1978 Don was the first Johansen to win the Canadian Bull Riding Championship and went on to the National Finals in Oklahoma. In 1979 Jack and Bruce joined Don in qualifying for the Canadian finals, but Jack was forced to withdraw due to a shoulder injury.

In 1980 Bruce became the second brother to win the Canadian Championship. Dale soon followed, winning back to back championships in '83 and '84. He was a contestant at the National Finals Rodeo four times and won the $50 000 jackpot at the Calgary Stampede twice. In 1987 Guy was the last Johansen brother to become the Canadian Bull Riding Champion.

Numerous times, before and after I met Jack, people told me that I had to talk to the Johansen brothers. They are not only respected for their bull riding skills and as bull riding instructors, but for who they are as people. I hadn't been steered wrong.

"How did you guys get so good?" I ask.

"Well, what happened was that one year Dad got hailed out. His whole crop was destroyed, so there was no grain to put in the Quonset, so he converted it into a bull riding arena. All winter long we'd get on 100 bulls, then we would ride another 100 during the summer.

"We rode every Wednesday and Sunday. During the winter we'd heat the Quonset with a coal heater. After we rode the bulls, we'd play broom ball, so we'd be all sweated up." Then they'd have to go out in the cold prairie night. A great way to catch a chill.

Jack smiles at a thought. "On Sundays the Hutterites would come to watch us. They couldn't do anything on Sunday except worship, so they'd get dressed up, get in their three ton truck and drive over to watch us ride the bulls."

Wife Glenda listens, and adds her perspective, filling in details. They have two boys, Calvin and Mark. Calvin didn't take to riding bulls, but Mark is a steer rider.

"They were all young, and travelled together," Glenda adds. "There was Jim Brown, Bronc Stott and Kevin Larsen. They had too much fun."

When Jack married, he decided it was time to quit bull riding and settle down, but he didn't get out of the sport. All five brothers had a role to play in making the Strathmore Dodge Ram Tough Bull Riding Classic happen and they have the Johansen Brothers Bull Riding School, which they started in 1978. They have helped develop some of Canada's top bull riders. Jeff Keeley, Wes Cyr and Jeff Whitlow (who had just scored the 90 pt. ride) have all been to their school.

"You know how to pick them."

"No, we don't pick them," Jack responds. "They come to us. The school is open to anyone."

The three day session runs in March and costs $375. The riders are taught the basics and they ride 7 to 12 bulls. More recently the Johansen brothers started a steer riding school. "Kids coming out of our school have made the Canadian Finals," Jack says.

"What do you teach them?"

"The basics. How to get on, how to get off. It's the same as sending a kid to a hockey school. They have to get all the basics. If they have the heart and the try, they will make it as bull riders."

"What makes a man a good bull rider?"

"He's gotta have heart."

I take a lot of Jack's time and he is very patient with my questions, coming from a position of almost complete ignorance about his sport.

I stand alone writing notes on what he had told me when Jay comes over.

"We've got tickets for the dance at the arena. You wanna come? We got a ticket for you too if you want it."

"Sure."

"But if you come you have to go to Cereal with us tomorrow."

"You're my ride."

"I guess you're going to Cereal then," he grins at me.

I have no idea where Cereal is, except it is somewhere near the Saskatchewan border and I have no idea where I'm going to sleep. I wasn't at all worried about it.

Weekend Whisky

We all walk back to the Oldsmobile, the sun is gone, but the lazy Alberta sunset continues to linger on the horizon.

We are joined by Kelly McEwan. He squeezes into the back seat in the middle with Shelly at one door, me at the other. Kelly and his ride are going in different directions; he has to ride slack at Cereal in the morning, so he is going with us.

We drive over to the curling rink where the dance is being held. Weekend Whiskey is playing to a mixed crowd of cowboys and townies, and even some people who'd come out from Calgary. Most were dressed in jeans and shirts, lots of cowboy hats, and there are some motley looking guys who don't fit the cowboy image. No one is about to ask them to leave.

The long curling rink, minus the ice, is dark, except for the ends. At one end the band is set up behind a dance floor. At the opposite end is the bar. In between are long wooden tables and chairs filled with earnest people talking to each other, except for groups of young ladies dressed to catch the attention of the young men. Amazingly enough they sit alone, undisturbed by any romancers, for most of the evening. It takes awhile for things to heat up.

The place is full, a sell out, and it's noisy. I get a Coors, it's all they are offering in terms of beer, and I slump down in one of the few available chairs. I'm tired. It's been a hell of a long day. I'm really happy with it, but I just want to sit and drink beer, even if it is only Coors.

Clint tells me a story about a time he was in Victoria, staying with a friend. "I'd been out drinking and we were walking home and I was almost to my friend's place when I saw him drive by, really slowly. He was very drunk. Right behind him was a cop car, and I was sure they were going to pull him over, which they did. I thought, I'm going to have to do something to help him out, so I walk over and kick the cop car.

"'What you doing?' they ask me.

"'Kicking your car,' I said and gave it another kick.

"They got out and said, 'If you're going to keep kicking the car we're going to have to arrest you.'

"I said, 'Then arrest me.'

"So they throw us into the back of the cop car and they drove us around for awhile. We talked with them and we were getting along quite well with them, but then they took us and threw us in the drunk tank. My friend got arrested anyways, so my efforts went for nothing."

"What were you doing?" Shelly is laughing at him.

"I thought I was creating a diversion," he grins.

"He's full of hot air," Shelly says. "He's just like his Dad. You can play a joke on him and he'll believe you."

Clint protests, but Shelly is still teasing him, "A cowboy has got to be smarter than his shirt," she chides.

Chad Wakefield before his ride at Nanton.

Sitting next to me is Vance Keith from Entwistle, Alberta. He and his family are into horse urine, which they get from the fillies. He explains the process, which requires collecting the urine at the right time of the month. They sell it to cosmetic companies in Europe. It's a big business.

Sitting across from me is a pert young blonde. Shelly introduces us. "This is Shelly, yes she's Shelly too. He's writing a book about bull riders."

Shelly's eyes light up. "This is Chad Wakefield. Chad's got a lot of stories to tell." Chad is not big, not even for a bull rider, but he has those clean good looks that attract not only the young girls, but has gotten him into the movies. Later in the evening, he gets up and sings with the band. He is planning on going to Nashville to start a music career.

"What are you going to call the book?" he asks.

"Bull."

He frowns and leans back in his chair. "It makes us sound like we're full of bull."

"I thought of it as being more of a powerful name, like the power of the bull," I reply.

"Naw. You should call it something else."

"What do you suggest?"

He sits leaning back, beer can in hand, thinking, then he says, "Twister."

By Shelly's reaction, I can tell she doesn't think that's a good name.

"People will think it's about a storm or something," I reply.

"A good bull is a twister," Chad responds.

"Chad's got a lot of good stories," Shelly bubbles with energy and she grins from ear to ear.

But Chad's stories aren't immediately forthcoming. Chad looks away. "You should talk with Kevin West. He won Calgary in '88. He would've been one of the best. He has a lot more stories than I can tell. He remembers everything. He's a good guy to get information from. He was a really good friend when I was starting."

I'm leaning across the table trying to hear everything he says, which isn't easy with the band playing and the increasing noise from the several hundred people all talking, and all getting louder as the evening moves along.

"When did you start riding?" I ask.

"When I was 15."

"How old are you now?"

He says 27, but he looks much younger. "I don't do much riding now. I've been injured for the last year and haven't been able to ride much."

"Are you good?"

"I haven't made a lot of money at it," he replies. He is distant, and harder than his baby face looks would lead you to suspect. But he's been going down the road for a long time and has seen a lot of the seedier side of the rodeo, which is what he's probably thinking when he warns me off making the riders look like "dinks."

"I miss the travelling," he says. "It's the lifestyle and it's all the buddies and the places you go. And it's the friendship and camaraderie. You don't get that in other sports. As a bull rider you are on your own. There is no team and no coaches. You've got no one to blame or bitch about.

"From the age of 15 I've been going to the dances and watching the guys and being part of the life. I've seen TVs thrown through hotel windows and guys being fucked in campers and hotel rooms. It's about being in south Texas and having a $100 to your name and you've got to decide if you are going to use that money to go home or go to the next rodeo. You go to the next rodeo.

"One time I was in Rapid City, South Dakota, and I had $35. I had to borrow money to pay the entry fee. I scored 60-some points, so won the $100 day money. Instead of going home I went south and kept on rodeoing.

"One time I was in Dalton, Texas, and I had a stroke of luck."

Reading through my notes and trying to recall the conversation, I've yet to figure where the "stroke of luck" fits into this story.

Chad continues, "I got stepped on by a bull and it punctured my lung. When I was in hospital, I phoned my Dad and he sent me a plane ticket to go home with. But I couldn't fly for two weeks. Dean Fenton came and picked me up and we cashed in the plane ticket and went to Fort Worth, where we stayed at Scott Mendez's house. I was on my own a lot and Dean continued to rodeo. We were so broke that we could only eat once a day. We'd go to a place called What a Burger, where they had huge burgers that were really great. That'd be our meal for the day.

"There's no security to it all," Chad is intense. "You're young and you're 2000 miles away from home and you're wondering what's going to happen. Other guys come from big ranches (Chad is from Calgary) and it's no problem for them. Their parents can help them out. But my parents weren't in a position to be able to do that all the time. I had to look after myself."

Despite being hurt a lot, spending long periods in the hospital, being down on his luck and experiencing the danger up close and personal didn't put Chad off. "The danger is the furthest thing from these guys' minds," he says. "If you're going to think about it all the time you might as well stay at home. If I go to the rodeo and I'm thinking about getting bucked off and getting hurt, chances are 50/50 I'm going to get bucked off and get hurt."

"You've been hurt a lot. Why do you keep getting back on?"

"It's the lifestyle. You get there and you've got things in your head and you go out and do what you're suppose to do. I've been in the hospital more times than I can count. I'm lying there wondering what the fuck am I doing. But it is pride. You don't want them to beat you. There are not many guys out there that can go out and making a living riding bulls.

"Everybody I talk to these days is a broke dick. They can't afford to do it, but they keep doing it."

Chad persists, despite the difficulties.

"I was never very good," Chad states. "The best year I had was 30th in Canada."

(Later I was talking to Austin Beasley and mentioned that Chad didn't think he was much of a bull rider. "He was a good rider," Austin replied. "But he was hurt so much he was never able to ride at his best.")

"So what are you going to do now that your rodeo career is over?"

"I'm getting into movies. I'm going to work on *Eaters of the Dead*, then I'm going to Nashville and try to get into the music business. I do a lot of singing and songwriting. I've got to start making a living. You can only have fun for so long."

I laugh at this. "You can only have fun for so long." None of what he's been telling me sounds like any fun at all.

"You got any good travelling stories?"

He's reluctant to talk, but he huddles with Shelly for a while and then he reluctantly leans forward and says, "I'll tell you what going down the road is like. It's crazy.

"It was me and Wade Joyal, Joe Young Jr. and Dennis Koestler. It's November, the last part of November and it's -20 or so. We left Calgary heading for Regina. Wade's got new tires on his van and an hour out of Calgary, he blew a tire. We put the spare on and continue on our way. We get an hour from Regina and another tire blew. It was 40 below and we were freezing. We're standing out on the highway trying to get a ride and finally some steer wrestlers pick us up.

"We get to the rodeo and we're all bucked off. Nothing happened. Nobody wins nothing.

"So Jay Manning gives us a ride in his piece of shit car. We're trying to find a place to stay and we stop at a bar and get a drink and we're trying to pick up girls but nobody has any luck. It's a real bad night. Nothing is going right.

"We get back in the car and Joe's driving and he's driving like an idiot, he's doing donuts in the middle of the road. We yell at him that he's going to get us killed. Another couple saw us driving like that and they stopped at a gas station and they called the cops on us.

"I took over driving and I'm supposed to go out to Jay's house out in the country in the middle of the winter, and I don't know where I'm going. We've got directions and I've got about an 1/8th of a tank of gas and were trying to make it to Jay Manning's. We hit the ditch so we all get out and push our way out. We get back in the car and again I hit the ditch and this time I floor it and we get out. I know we're not going to make it to Jay's. It's dark and its cold and I've got directions, but I can't find it. Finally I get back to the highway and I pull into a rest stop. I pull the car over, it's too late to get to Jay's so we just all sleep in the car. We're out there on the frozen prairie, no heater in the car. It's crazy.

"We wake up in the morning and we decide to go and get the van and get it fixed. In the night Joe Young had to piss. He was in the back seat and he pissed in his sleep over the front seat onto Dennis' head. We laughed our heads off. Everybody was okay about it. Dennis wasn't too pissed off."

Chad trails off. The story is finished but he doesn't seem to know how to wrap it up. It's not a story with a punch line, it is a sketch of the life going down the road. "We could've died out there. It's crazy, but that's what it's like when you're going down the road. Sometimes nothing works out. We go all that way, nobody gets anything, we don't even pick up any girls.

"If I had a daughter, that's one place I wouldn't let them go," Chad adds. "I wouldn't let them hang around the bull riders."

"They don't settle down until they're 30," Shelly puts in.

"Chad!" someone yells at him. "The band wants you to go sing."

I want to listen to him, but Shelly starts telling me how they met.

"I was sitting in the Ranchmans minding my own business when he bumped into me and nearly knocked me over," she speaks quickly, spilling over like champagne, leaning across the table talking above the noise.

"'You're kind of pretty,' he says. I said 'Fuck off and quit bumping into me.' But he kept talking, so I thought I'd give him a chance. He told me that he was riding next at Big Stone. Then he said, 'I'll give you a call tomorrow.'

"I said 'Bullshit! I bet you $10 bucks you don't call me.' 'You're on,' he says.

"So a month goes by and I don't hear anything from him and then I go to Airdrie and I go behind the chutes and he was standing there and I called 'Chad Wakefield' and he looks at me and he says 'Shelly Aaskow.'

"'I just came to collect the $10 you owe me.'

"'How about I buy you out in beer instead?'

"I said, 'Okay.' That's how we met. That was two years ago.'"

"Are you going to get married?"

"No!" she snaps at me. It's a touchy question.

I chat with Vance Keith, who is sitting to my left and I'm introduced to Quinn Franklin and his girlfriend, Robyn Hines. The music plays on and Jay and Clint are off talking to people and Kelly sits down the end of the table. Shelly comes and goes, checking in on me every once in awhile. I get another beer.

Quinn and Robyn huddle together across the table, whispering. "Tell him, maybe he'll put it in the book," Robyn urges him. Quinn doesn't want to talk. He has a long gentle face and a very shy smile. Looking at him you wouldn't think he made his living in the most dangerous sport in North America. Robyn and I urge him on and finally he says, "Okay. I've only got one story. It's not much of a story."

"Don't worry about it."

He leans across the table, "One time there was a bull riding at Wolf Creek and after it was over we went to Billy Bob's in Red Deer. They were holding a wet t-shirt contest that night and it got pretty wild. The cowboys started to fight with the townies. I didn't fight, I was really drunk, but I didn't get in the fight. At the time I had a little Ranger with a topper on it. It was parked out in the parking lot. Someone else had the key so I couldn't drive it, so I crawled in the back and went to sleep.

"The cops come along and they arrest me for sleeping in my truck."

"Get outta here." I couldn't believe that. People camp in their vehicles all the time. It was a lot better having a drunk sleep it off in the back of his truck then trying to drive somewhere to sleep.

"I wasn't driving or anything, just sleeping. They arrested five of the cowboys and four townies and they put them all in jail. So I'm in jail with these guys and some of them still want to fight. This big guy was really angry and he was shouting at me, telling me 'you'd better shut up'. I thought I was going to get beat up in the jail cell.

"I slept for a few hours on the cement before they let me out. Another guy they had arrested for pissing in the parking lot."

Then he finished it off. "That's my story," he says.

"How did you do today?" I ask.

"Today I was mad at myself. I rode him for seven seconds and you're not suppose to get bucked off then. Today it just didn't . . . some days it just doesn't go well. But I guess if it was easy, everyone would do it."

"Why do you do it?"

"Why do guys parachute? Or go downhill skiing, which I think is more dangerous. When you do a good ride it is the best feeling in the world. You know you've tried hard and you've done well so that's a good feeling."

Shelly Aaskow leans over, "They are really cute guys, but they are retarded."

Quinn and Clint protest, but not strongly.

"If you want to talk to retards, talk to wild horse racers. They are really crazy." Then she goes off in search of Chad.

"You get nervous watching him ride?" I ask Robyn.

"No, but I don't particularly like it though. Mostly I get nervous about him doing well. In the back of my head I guess I worry about him getting hurt, but more I just want to see him get a good mark. I did see him get hung up once, but not really serious."

Was it style or luck, I don't know, but Quinn, who's been a professional for five years and started riding much younger, hasn't had the serious injuries that have put Chad in the hospital more times than he can remember.

Maybe Robyn gave me a clue when she said, "Quinn knows every bull in his head. He knows their trip, knows which way they're going to go."

A middle-aged lady in a baseball cap stands behind Quinn and puts her hand on his shoulder, "Quinn is one of the nicest guys that has ever walked the face of the earth," she says sincerely.

"Who are you?" I take a drink of beer, and it's been a long time between drinks. I'm tired of writing. I want to put my pen away and just relax and finish the beer, but I don't get the chance.

"I'm a stock contractor's wife." I can't see her face as it is in shadows under the baseball cap she is wearing and the light is behind her. I think she's the lady that was taking care of the gate this evening, but I don't know for sure.

"What kind of a book are you writing?" she demands. When I tell her, she says, "What are you going to call it?"

"Bull."

"Perfect!" she says enthusiastically. She gets into a discussion over the name with Chad, who has returned and is sitting across from me again. Shelly is standing next to him.

"There are a lot of stories these guys can tell you. After awhile you get to hear the same ones over and over again, and it isn't so interesting anymore. I've been around these young men for a long time. I know them all."

"Who are you?" I ask again.

"Just say I'm a stock contractor's wife. I know of where I speak," she leans over the table and talks in my ear.

As I write this, she straightens and lights a cigarette, then she suddenly grabs my notebook from my hand and reads what I've just written. It is not particularly funny, but she whoops with laughter and everyone turns to look. Now they want to know what I've written and I finally get a break from writing as my notebook is handed about. No one else sees the humor.

"These guys are great," she says. "You go to these things and you don't see any drugs. Sure they drink, but they are pretty clean living," she's yelling in my ear again.

"Who's your husband?" I ask, but she won't tell me.

"He's well known around here. He's got three kids and he thinks no less of his bulls than he does of the kids. You shouldn't put that in. It might give people the wrong impression. He's a good father, but he really does like his bulls."

She goes off and comes back with a drink. Before she has the opportunity to drink it, she is asked to dance.

"You watch that drink for me," she clears a place amongst the empties for it, and there are a lot of empties stacked on the table.

"Will do," I assure her, and lean back and relax. It's now 12:15.

"Okay, let's go," Clint comes along. "We gotta get out of here."

I'm willing to go. In fact, I would've leapt right up had it not been for the drink I was suppose to be watching.

Jay and Kelly don't seem to be in a rush to leave. Shelly Jones isn't around.

"Come on, guys, we've got to get out of here. Floyd, let's go."

I stand up. The stock contractor's wife comes back so she can look after her own drink. I head for the car where Shelly is already asleep in the backseat. I get in, then Kelly gets in and I'm stuck in the middle, sitting over the tranie with my backpack crammed between my knees. Kelly and Shelly are taking up all the good space.

Jay and Clint get in the front and the discussion begins about where we are going to stay. We're also joined by a girl who lives in Strathmore and she sits in the front and directs us to a local hotel.

Kelly doesn't want to stay in town. He wants to get closer to Cereal so it won't be such a long drive for him in the morning.

"Don't worry. We'll get up early. You'll get there on time," Clint assures him.

Kelly isn't assured. "It's going to be another $60 cab ride," he says.

When we arrive at the hotel, it becomes a moot point, as it's full.

"We'll go to Drumheller."

Clint and Jay are tired and don't want to make the long drive.

I can see Kelly's point. It is easy to say one thing the night before, but when you wake up in the morning, after a short, alcohol-enhanced snooze, you're not quite as perky as you were the night before.

We drop the girl off at a bar. As we drive around, Kelly offers to drive. It's already getting on towards 12:40 or so. We find an open gas station and we go in and buy some munchies, get gas and start for the highway.

"Which way do we go? Left or right?" No one knows for sure.

I'm sitting on the hump. Shelly is already curled up and sleeping. Kelly is marking his territory. I'm sitting up straight with little choice but to watch the road ahead.

The decision is made to go back towards Calgary, where we'll find a highway going north.

Jay is driving and I'm in a quandary. I'd like to talk to Jay, just to keep him awake, but if I talk to him he's going to look over his shoulder at me. He's already dog tired. However, Clint talks with him, so I relax, or try to. The road stretches straight out before us in an unbroken line, illuminated in the near distance while blackness encloses us on all sides. The lights of Calgary loom before us until we get to the intersection and turn north.

Sleep is impossible, for me. We race through the night. Kelly and Shelly sleeping, Jay and Clint chatting in the front seat and me sitting straight up, squeezed on both sides, my head feeling as if it was stuffed with cotton, my eyes wide open. For too long I'm like this.

Finally I doze, not too far from reality, when the sudden deceleration of the car brings me out of the fog. Jay pulls over and he changes places with Clint. I didn't learn until the next morning the reason Clint took over. Jay had started drifting to the edge of the highway. "I wasn't asleep," he said. He held his hands like they were holding the steering wheel, "I was watching us drive off the road."

We don't go off the road, but continue on. I'm numbed into unconsciousness for a few minutes before we reach Drumheller. We wait in the car while Clint goes in to see if there is a room available.

There isn't.

Kelly gets his wish. We're heading for Hanna, where there is supposed to be a vacancy at the Flying Goose.

We whip out of the parking lot and find ourselves on the wrong side of the divided highway. There's no traffic. The Olds navigates the fortunately low island with little problem. We wind through Drumheller, which is in a valley. The road snakes up a steep incline before getting on the open flat prairie again where the speedometer edges up to the top end. I'm overtired and still find it hard to sleep. I'm just hoping Clint is feeling better than I am.

It's 3:00 am when we finally get to Hanna, and there is a room at the motel. There's a huge Canada goose, wings extended, on the front lawn.

We get a room with two double beds. I immediately claim the floor and Jay tosses me a blanket from his bed and Clint gives me the matching one from his. I don't have to fight anyone else off who wants to take the floor.

I make a pillow out of my shirt. It's not uncomfortable and I sleep soundly.

He's quiet, sensitive and serious. A man you can identify with.

Cereal Rodeo Announcer

A Bowl of Cereal

When I wake up, Kelly is already gone. He took the car and went to ride slack in Cereal. It's about 8:00 or so. I can't get back to sleep, so I get up and shower. I'd hoped that the shower would give me some life, but it doesn't. When I left my sister's the morning before I expected to be back home that evening, so I didn't pack a toothbrush or razor blade. I have a lot of things in my backpack but none of them to do with personal hygiene. I put on my grubby, dusty clothes. I'm feeling wretched.

The others are still sleeping, so I go to the motel restaurant. I figure I better eat a good meal to get me through the day. If today is like other days I can't predict when and what I will eat next.

I order an omelet and gratefully drink the coffee, and the waitress keeps refilling it and I drink cup after cup until my eyes begin to float, but it doesn't make me feel any better. I'm not hung over. I only drank two beer at the dance. When the omelet arrives I pick at it, but can't eat it. I eat the toast and the slices of orange and tomato that come with it, but I can't get the omelet past my lips.

I write for over an hour, expecting to be joined by the others any minute. They don't come. I give up trying to eat the omelet. It's gone cold and I go outside to take a look at what there is to see, which isn't much. The small town, Sunday morning feeling, with everyone going to church, scares me back inside. I sit in the lobby for a while, still feeling not too good.

About 11:00 I go back to the room and Jay and Shelly and Clint are awake, making moves like they are about to get up.

I return to the café and they join me shortly after.

"No sign of Kelly yet?"

"No."

They eat breakfast without any problem.

"How much was the room?" I ask.

"$60.00."

"Divided by five," I say.

Jay shakes his head, "I thought we should divide it by four."

Clint doesn't like that, "Why should you get a deal because you are a couple?"

"I didn't mean us," Jay nods in my direction. "He slept on the floor and . . ."

"I figured I should pay more," I interrupt him. "I didn't have anyone crowding my space or trying to hog the blankets."

We split the bill five ways.

They finish eating and time is moving on, it's well past noon. The Cereal Rodeo starts at 1:30 and Kelly isn't back yet.

We joke about what's happened to him.

"He probably finished riding then headed on to the next rodeo. He's probably half way to Morris by now," I suggest.

They aren't worried. The bull riding is the last event so they still have lots of time.

At ten to one Kelly arrives and we get ready to leave.

I'm waiting at the car when Clint and Jay come out toting their rigging bags. Jay is giving Clint the gears for trying to pick up a girl the night before. "That was the best effort for the worst girl," Jay chides him. "You should have your pecker smacked."

Clint isn't about to take that. Shelly and Jay must have had a little spat. Clint asks what the matter with her is.

Jay says it's nothing.

"You're proving what we all know, that you can't go down the road and take a girl with you."

Jay throws his bag into the trunk of the car.

"You're proving that you can't even do it for one day," Clint's bag goes in next to his.

If there are any bad feelings between Jay and Shelly, they don't show it.

"What took you so long?" Kelly is asked as we get out on the highway.

"Aw, everything took longer than it should've. They weren't very organized, and then a cowboy got hurt and we had to wait for the ambulance."

"They didn't have an ambulance?"

"Yeah, they did, but they had to wait for the other one to return. They couldn't start the rodeo when there was no ambulance there."

"It's going to be a dust bowl," Jay warns me.

We're travelling fast, the flat prairie rushing past us, but we get slowed down by Sunday traffic; large holiday campers and trucks with trailers, and Cereal seems a long way away.

This is God's country. There is a feeling that out here there is room for God in all this space under this immense sky. In the city God seems to get squeezed out by the buildings and traffic and noise, but here there is room for Him to roam.

Out here the values are different. When we arrive at Cereal the announcer is talking about the "Christian fellowship" they enjoyed that morning.

"He's quiet, sensitive and serious," he describes a cowboy who is about to ride. "A man you can identify with."

Folk are sitting around the arena in their lawn chairs. There are stands, but they do little to enclose this unbridled exuberance of space. There are two kiosks. At one hot dogs and hamburgers, fries and sodas are for sale. At the other, ice cream and milkshakes. Shelly tells me the milkshakes are good.

The air is thirsty, the wind scrubbing my face, distilling all moisture. Persistently, the elements are unrelenting. We find shelter in thin slices of shade. A broken old windmill in the adjacent museum refuses to be moved by the wiles of the wind.

I want to find out about the history of Cereal. What kind of a town it is. I go into the rodeo office, where several gentlemen are sitting around, but they can't tell me much. It is the 20th anniversary of the rodeo. The town goes back to 1910, I'm told. They say it got its start further out from its present location. 'Further out' from the railway. It was moved to where it is now when the railway went through.

"What's the population?"

"About 200, including cats and dogs."

"What's the most interesting thing about Cereal?"

"Watching the sidewalks roll up at night." They laugh, but there isn't much they can tell me about the town.

With 300 paying customers, the entire town and then some is at the rodeo.

Dave Leader is here. "I've been telling the guys what you are doing. You want to talk to any of them and they'll be glad to help you."

I appreciate that. I feel less like an outsider, less like an old horse in a pen full of bulls. Some of the riders recognize me and nod or say hello.

I wander around behind the chutes. A horse is really acting up in the chute and the cowboy is pulled off just before the horse falls down, crumpled up in the confined space. A big cowboy hops on the ramp and hauls off and punches the horse in the jaw. Sufficiently chastised, the horse rights itself, gets square on its feet and behaves. He goes out in the arena and gives a good performance. Then the horse in the next chute starts misbehaving and it gets the same treatment. Justice is swift and direct. And effective.

It's a long wait for the bull riding. The cowboys are pacing quietly, edgy, behind the chutes. Cars race by on the highway, a cold indifference to the private dramas being played out here. Being behind the chutes, walking amongst them, I can feel their desire to ride and do well. I feel the tension. I don't know for sure, but I doubt whether they could be more tense now than at Calgary. The purse here can't be one of the bigger ones. Last night at Strathmore, the riders seemed more relaxed.

They are all there together, alone in their minds, as they prepare to ride. To make their money, or not. It's the smallest of the rodeos I've been to, but the danger is the same. Each bull has the potential to do as much damage to a man here in Cereal as it does in Calgary. A bull rider's reputation may not be made in Cereal, but he can be broken here. Most of the rodeos are small. There are few the size of Calgary, and more the size of Cereal. The riders put in their best effort every time out.

"Let's get her hot boys," the chute boss calls.

Riders are going through the motions, free hand up, jerking back and forth. A bull kicks and kicks and bangs around in the chute. They will be coming together in a matter of moments.

"Don't the cowboys look good the way they get all dressed up to get messed up?" the announcer says. "They all wear the same deodorant. It smells like Absorbine Junior."

Jay is getting on his bull. He's taking his time. His eyes are intense. He isn't smiling now. Standing at the chutes, I can see and feel the power of the bull, and I'm not sitting astride him.

The bull bursts out into the arena and Jay rides him well, but he is disqualified. His free hand brushed the bull, according to the judge sitting on the fence in front of where I'm standing.

Jay walks back through the arena and the judge asks him if he touched the bull. Jay smiles and says he did and keeps walking. Later, when the bucking is over, Bernie Bowe yells at Jay, "Did you *pet* him Jay!? Did you *pet* that bull? Don't tell me you were *petting* him!"

"No, I didn't touch him," Jay says.

But he wouldn't say that to the judge. It is part of the code, you accept what you are given.

"I've slapped 9 or 10 bulls this year. This one was pretty easy. He was young and didn't have the power to throw me. Not like the one I had last night."

Clint gets bucked along the fence and comes down heavily. He walks over to where I'm watching from.

"What happened?"

"He was bucking good, but he got into the fence, then he threw me off. I should've rode him," he takes out his package of snuff and takes a chew. "But it's things like that that keep a guy honest. Reminds you that it's not easy."

Dave has got a rank and powerful bull. It is moving before the gate is open. Right out of the chute it leaps up and turns to the left and Dave is airborne, hitting the dirt on the right.

Bernie is sympathetic and says to Dave as he comes off, "God couldn't've made that corner."

I ask Dave about that. "No, I should've rode him, but I overanticipated him. Sometimes it is not good to think too much about what you are going to do. I didn't have left on my mind. I expected him to go right. If I'd been there I would've rode him. I didn't even get warmed up. He probably didn't know I was riding him. Like golf, this is a humbling sport. He pulled me around a little more than I was expecting him to. I was riding him like he was a 100 point bull and he was only an 85. I was overanxious and he pulled me around and if I hadn't overanticipated I would've been with him."

There is a break in the action. I talk with Doug Groves, the clown, and Karen Lane, his fiancée. They tell me to come to the hospitality tent after the rodeo and they'll tell me some good stories. Unfortunately I don't make it, as Dave Leader offers me a ride, and like me, he's in a hurry to get back to Calgary. I was supposed to have dinner with my brother and his family, and I still have the foolish idea that I can make it on time.

Clint puts ice on his elbow. He had it operated on the year before and it still gives him trouble.

"How did you do?" one rider asks another.

"I released the beast," he responds.

"You mean you got tossed."

"Yeah."

The Bitter End

Bernie Bowe contemplates his future after being bucked off at Cereal.

One cowboy gets bucked and he comes out of the arena and throws his rope on the ground. He's really upset.

Bernie Bowe gets bucked and he comes off feeling much the same way. He's angry, but he controls himself. He looks like he wants to go over and kick the fence, but he doesn't.

I walk over to the semi-trailer that serves as a change room for the cowboys. It is simply an enclosed space where they can have a bit of privacy, but most cowboys change out in the open.

Bernie's laying on the ground, his back against the fence, he looks very despondent, head propped against the lower rail of the pen. I take his picture and he nods.

I'm reluctant to approach him. He's had a rough day and he might not feel like answering any questions. But he does. He's not upset just because he's had one bad ride. There is more to it than that.

"It's the end for me," he says. "I'm out of money, so I've got to go back to work. It's a bitter end." The 37-year-old from Hinton, Alberta, has been riding for 21 years and this is the first time that he has had to stop rodeoing in the middle of the season.

"This is the first time that I've had to go back to work because I've run out of money. It is a bitter pill to swallow," he's in a black mood.

Bernie moves oil rigs for a living. He spends two weeks in the bush then has one week out.

Dave Leader, who worked for eight years on the rigs, says, "Working on the rigs makes you pretty hungry for riding bulls. When you spend eight months in the bush, it makes riding bulls seem pretty easy."

There are three main reasons that bull riders quit going down the road, and no matter which reason forces them to quit, there is usually a feeling of dissatisfaction. They'd like to be riding the bulls into their mid 90s. If not longer.

Injuries will knock a man out. Either one serious injury which makes him think about what he is doing or disables him. Or having nagging injuries which give him constant pain and affect his ability to ride will also bring him to the decision it's time to leave the rigging bag in the closet. Even after the rider has been injured, they don't always pack up the rosin right away. They are determined to show that they have healed up, that they don't fear the beast, that they've still got it, and they go back and ride again. And sometimes they do their best riding after they've been injured. But some don't last much longer. They might do another year, prove to themselves what they need to, and then retire.

Marriage doesn't always take the man out of the circuit, but having a wife and a kid makes a man think about his responsibility to people other than himself. Travelling puts a constant strain on relationships. When the guys are travelling, they are on the road for extended periods of time. It is not a case of going to a rodeo, going home, going to the next rodeo, going home. They go from rodeo to rodeo to rodeo, and it is not always easy to keep in contact with the family when they are riding in the afternoon then getting behind the donut and travelling all night to get to the next place. Arriving, catching some sleep, eating and riding again in the afternoon before hitting the road once more.

The drinking, hanging out in bars and the interest of women in bull riders certainly does nothing to promote stable relations. Without a doubt, for whatever reasons, there are women who are attracted to the bull riders, and they are generally not shy about making their interest known.

Going broke is another good reason for quitting, but it's usually the last thing that will force the cowboy to quit. And that is only when the hard cold reality hits them that they are not making any money and they have no choice but to work. The bull riders will put up with a lot before they finally get to this point. They will sell what they own, borrow from friends and family, and go without food. They sleep wherever they can find a place and pray that they have a good ride at the next rodeo so they can continue on.

As the athletes become more professional, treating their sport like a sport, training for it, keeping in shape, working when they work and limiting the diversions, they are also giving more consideration to what they are doing when they are not rodeoing, and what they are going to do when their career comes to an end. The top riders can earn a good living riding bulls, but you don't have to go too far down in the standings before the bull riding money isn't enough on its own to keep body and soul together. These riders have a second and sometimes a third occupation.

The Darker Side

It's been a long day in the sun and wind at Cereal. I buy a milkshake, the first thing I've eaten since picking at my omelet this morning.

Jay, Clint, Kelly, their energy level seems down too. No one has done very well. Even Jay stops smiling, briefly. That's like having the sun set in the middle of the afternoon. Shelly has hardly left the shade of the trailer.

I begin to understand how difficult it can be to work and travel, and live the lifestyle these bull riders do. Going into Beirut hadn't been as difficult and covering the Peace Keeping Troops in Cambodia had been easy compared with this. I wasn't wiped out because of drinking. I hadn't drank that much and it would take more than a tin or two of Coors Light to give me a buzz. I didn't experience the tension or the physical danger the bull riders did, but I had to work hard. The interviews were exhausting as I stood on my feet concentrating on their every word and trying to make it all coherent.

Being in the elements and not eating well has not had a good effect on me either. I also feel bad about messing up the plans with my family. I haven't talked to my sister since leaving her place the morning before.

My brother Rex and his family had invited us all over for a barbecue, and I thought I might be able to make it back to Calgary on time to at least catch the tail end. But as the day went on, I realized I wouldn't be home until at least 8:00 p.m., and they would've eaten by then. If they'd been waiting for me for a long time, I might not want to show up at all.

I talk about this with Dave Leader as we drive across the prairie to Calgary. Messing up the family's plan is not an uncommon experience with bull riders. "I'm the one in my family who doesn't show up for family get-togethers," he says. "It's not always easy to make it. You're on the road and you can't get home when you planned."

I give him a copy of the glossary that I've written up from the information he gave me when we were in Williams Lake. I give him three pages and tell him he can keep them and let me know if there are any changes to be made. His pickup passes a slow moving motorhome, but then again, everything is moving slow compared to us.

He takes the pages and reads them as he's driving. He still drives better than Jay. He didn't once wander off the road.

"Looks fine," he says. He suggests one small change.

We talk about our lives as we watch what I think is an incredibly beautiful scene roll before our eyes. The fields alternate between the mustard yellow of the rapeseed to green fields of grain still growing. Farms that look if they were emblazoned on the canvas of a painter who views the world as an ideal, unspoilt Garden of Eden seem as much a part of nature as the groves of trees.

The light takes on a special hue as thick clouds paint a black swath across the western horizon. It is still miles away, but the jagged flashes of lightning cut yellow streaks against the dark sky.

The pickup drones on, racing towards the storm, which is crackling and thundering in its rush to wash over us. The rain comes in a deluge. Pounding the earth, bouncing off the highway. Lightning flashing in front of our eyes, thunder is breaking over our heads.

Dave doesn't slow down.

In many ways Dave is little different from other Canadians his age, but until he starts talking about another part of his nature, it wasn't evident in his easy-going manner.

"I think one of the reasons that bull riders get in a lot of trouble," he says, "is that in most situations you are not afraid. Your level of fear is a lot higher than what other people's is. Since we were kids we've lived in a tough atmosphere and it makes us a little harder than we should be."

He tells of a fight that illuminates the dark side of him. "We were in a bar and there was one guy who was looking for trouble. He was being a real jerk and was getting everyone riled up. We all went outside and everyone was fighting. But this guy who'd started it all took off. He really angered me and I wanted to get him so I went looking for him. I found him and we were in the parking lot, but he was way taller than me, and he outweighed me. We had grabbed each other and there was no way I could hit him because his arms were way longer than mine.

"I had a minute to think about things. We're standing there facing each other, with a good grip on each other. I couldn't do much so I head-butted him. He went down and out. I'd hit him right in the nose. It happened so fast that nobody saw what happened.

"The police had arrived. And the original guys that were in the fight got a face full of pepper spray, which took all the mustard out of them." It took Dave a little longer to settle down and a scuffle with a police officer finally brought matters to an end.

We stop in Drumheller for a milkshake and he phones a lady he is going out for dinner with when he gets back to Calgary. He's smiling broadly when he gets off the phone. "We're having Indian food at her place."

Dave doesn't want to tell me about her; she is an actress working on the movie that he's doing stunts for, and doesn't want the word to get out that they are seeing each other. Bull riding is a safer topic.

"When I'm riding a lot," Dave says, "I get sore and it puts you off a bit, you don't ride as well as you can. But I'm not riding as much anymore and so I feel a lot better, but when I don't ride so much I lose a little bit of my edge."

"Do you practice?"

"No, I don't need to practice any more."

In Calgary he drops me off at the C-train parking lot and my car is still there, untouched. I get back to my sister's to find that dinner at my brother's has been called off, and it's not all my fault, so I can face them again. I go off to a local restaurant and have dinner by myself.

Where Does the Money Go?

I take Monday off, and it seems like the rest of the days of the week want equal treatment. Nothing seems to go right. My computer breaks down. I try, once again, to get a pass into the Stampede from Brian Ratcliffe, and once again he refuses. He seems to be doing all that he can to make sure Calgary gets as little mention in the book as possible. When I mention this to him, he raises his hands in a "well, it can't be helped" gesture and says, "Well, that happens."

Tuesday I go to the Pro Rodeo office, where they are very helpful but unwilling to broach some subjects. A number of cowboys have expressed concern about how much of a slice of the economic pie they are getting. The Calgary Shoot Out sounds like a great payday for the cowboys, which it is, but the amount, $50 000 for the winner, hasn't changed since it began. Nobody at the Rodeo Office or at the Stampede wants to talk about it. Even though the Association's primary responsibility should be to the cowboy, they don't seem interested in upsetting the Calgary Stampede, or the other rodeos.

Several times I phoned the Stampede and asked for numbers. Each time they promised to get back to me with the information, but they never did.

Another concern the cowboys have is insurance. Being injured as often and as severely as they are, it is understandable that this would be of utmost importance to them. Their association does provide insurance for the cowboys, which kicks in at differing levels of injury and disability. They could have higher coverage, but as Morgan Holbrook, Rodeo Administrator, explains, "The cowboys tend to be independent in their natures. They don't like to have a lot of administration interfering with what they do. They tend to like to take care of themselves and go their own way. We have insurance with a great variety of payouts, which is decided by the membership. They decide what level of coverage they are going to have."

I was leaving the office when two young cowboys come in. The secretary introduces me to Austin Beasley. I ask him what he's up to.

"I ride tomorrow at Calgary. If I do well, I'm going to stay home and rest up for the finals. If I don't, and I'm out of the money here, I'm going to drive down to Casper, Wyoming, and then to Sheraton, Wyoming. I should be back Friday or Saturday."

"Can I go with you?"

"Sure. If I go. I'm still not sure I'm going. Can you drive?"

"Yeah, of course."

"I'll get some use out of you then."

"Fine with me."

"I'll call you about 7:00 Wednesday evening if I'm going."

I was really looking forward to the opportunity to do some serious driving, but Wednesday evening Austin doesn't call. At 11:00 p.m. I watch the rodeo highlights on TV. Austin gets bucked and lands in front of the bull, which promptly buts him in the small of the back and roughs him up a little. I can see why he hasn't called. After that, he probably didn't feel like sitting 10 to 12 hours, driving through the night.

The Crossroads Motor Inn is one of the places the cowboys and their fans like to hang out. Thursday afternoon I pop in there and have no trouble picking out two guys who are playing pool who I'm sure are, or were, bull riders. And I'm right. Lonny Corbet and Tim Kotelniski are now retired, and though they had only made semi-pro, their stories and point of view are as interesting as the pro riders.

They are now both 27 years old and started riding at the same time.

"We did everything together. We started together, it was our adventure together. We've known each other since we were five," Tim wields his pool cue. He's from Delacour, Alberta, while Lonny's from Priddis.

"We grew up with going to the rodeos. I liked a lot of the events," Lonny says while Tim takes his shot. "But I chose bull riding because it is the most powerful of them all."

"And you don't have to fall as far as when you're bucked from a horse," Tim adds.

"Is it true that girls are more attracted to the bull riders than the other cowboys?"

"Yes, the girls like the bull riders," Lonny says, then adds with a hint of derision, "for some stupid reason."

"Because of the danger?"

"There's not a lot of danger," he sits down at the high bar table where I'm writing. But then he tells me about the injury he sustained in Olds when the bull stepped on him (There's no Pain Like It). "I went back to work after I got out of the hospital. I was lugging beef at the time," he adds, "Which was no easy task. But you do what you gotta do to make a living."

"Was it a tough decision to quite riding?"

"No," he takes a sip of beer. "It wasn't really a tough decision to make. I thought there was no sense getting myself killed if I wasn't going to make it to 'The Show.' The average career is six years, which I lasted. It was tough on the body. Some days I would wake up feeling like I was 45."

Me too, I thought, and I'm only 44.

Tim said though he had never been injured, he quit because he wasn't making any money. "When you're not making any money it's pretty hard, especially when you have a kid to feed."

"The top 20 bull riders are making good money, other than that there are a lot of guys not making any money. Now the money is beginning to compensate for the risks and the demands it makes on the cowboy, but when we were riding it was damned difficult to make a living."

They admit that they miss it a lot and if they were in shape and weren't in debt, they'd still be doing it. "It's the best rush you'll ever have," they both agree.

They went to Ty Northcott's bull riding school in Olds, where they teach you the basics, they video your ride and analyze what you did. "There are more Northcott bulls around than anyone else's," Lonny says.

Like all bull riders, they have their heroes, and they are familiar names. Lane Frost, Tuff Hedeman, Ty Murray, Donny Gaye and Jay Manning.

Not to diminish Jay's abilities, but I was surprised he was put in the same company with the World Champions. "Really?" I ask.

"Oh yeah, when Jay is on he rides like a wolf."

"Why was Frost so good?"

"He was just damned good. And he rode Red Rock."

"And Ty Murray?"

"Ty is from Stephenville, Texas. I named my son after him. Ty did it all. Bull riding, Bareback, Saddle Bronc and he went to the National Finals in all three events. That's pretty special. Ty won World All Round five times (1989-1994) and he was the youngest cowboy to reach a million dollars."

"If that was me," Tim injected, "I could still be riding."

Bodacious is the first name to come to mind when they are asked about great bulls. "He hurt too many guys," Lonny said. "Did you see what he did to Tuff Hedeman's face? It was not a pretty sight. The reason I admire Tuff is because he promised his son, that he named after Lane Frost, that he would never ride Bodacious again. At the Worlds in Vegas he drew Bodacious and he turned him out. I don't know if he would've won the Worlds or not, but by turning him out, he definitely couldn't win. That's a pretty special guy that will keep a promise like that for his son."

Are they thinking they would like to be able to do something equivalent for their sons?

"Oscar was a big old brave bull that wasn't rode too many times. For five or six years nobody rode him until Don Gay or Larry Mahan did. And Red Rock was a nasty bull. He'd take a hooking to you."

Today it is much easier to learn about the great riders and the bulls than it was. Lane Frost had a video out and Lonny and Tim watched tapes endlessly when they were starting. "I have about 100 tapes," Lonny explains. "We'd watch them and analyze them. It helps you to see what you can do. The bulls, eight out of ten times, will take the same trip. But they are athletes too, and they can have an off day. Just like a cowboy. I don't think they're mean. They don't want to kill you, they just want you off their back." Lonny is doing most of the talking.

"One trick the old timers used to do to get the bull to buck more would be to take an alligator clip and put it on the ear of the bull. It agitates them and makes them spin more. The judges like a bull that's spinning. But nobody does that anymore."

Their pool game is over and someone else takes over the table, but they are happy to continue talking and sipping beer.

"Another thing we did was we had an old barrel and we drilled holes in it, put some hooks in it and ran ropes through it. We hooked the ropes up to some trees and we'd shake the ropes around to get the motion of the bull. We'd have our own competitions."

Like all bull riders, Lonny and Tim think it is an unbeatable thrill. "The first time I rode," Lonny says, "I thought there was nothing like it. It was the best feeling in the world. Some guys like bungy jumping, some like sky diving, but I don't think they beat the thrill of bull riding. The first time I rode I was shaking like a leaf, but it's the greatest feeling in the world."

"The first time I rode," Tim relates, "it lasted about two seconds. The first time doesn't last very long."

Upon this bench have sat the greatest people in the world - the cowboys and their families. Sit a spell and add to the history of the Calgary Stampede.

Sign on bench outside the rodeo office at the Calgary Stampede

Jack Daines

Jack Daines is the size and shape of the barrel the rodeo clowns climb into when the bull takes a mind to mess with them. His voice is gravelly from years of doing auctions and announcing rodeos and, like most bulls, he can kick up some dirt, snort and tell you exactly what he wants you to know.

But he is a warm and friendly man with years of rodeoing experience that goes back to the days when he entered the Boys Steer Riding. He went from there to Novice Broncs, then Bull Riding and Saddle Bronc. He quit bull riding when he was 21. "I didn't get hurt," he growls, "I got married."

Jack continued Saddle Bronc riding until he realized he wasn't going to have a super career in the arena, so he decided to produce rodeos. In 1961

Jack Daines (right) has contributed a great deal to the rodeo in Alberta.

he started the rodeo at the Daines Ranch at Innisfail, Alberta, and has been producing quality rodeos ever since.

"In 1996 we were voted the best rodeo committee in Canada. That is the highest compliment that can be paid because it is voted on by the contestants," he states.

Two committees are so honored each year. One for "Over $2500 Added," which the Daines' rodeo won, and "Under $2500 Added," won by Luxton Rodeo in 1996.

It's Saturday morning and everyone is gathering outside the rodeo office behind the arena. And it is the final day of the regular rodeo events at the Calgary Stampede. Sunday is the final day and the day the $50 000 Shoot Out takes place. Today the stands will be overflowing and there is a feeling of excitement. Today is a big day, the winners will be decided.

Inside the media trailer I chat briefly with Bill Kehler who has been announcing rodeos since "1963 or '64. I've doing Calgary since '67," he says.

Everybody coming into the trailer says hello to Bill, who likes the attention. He's a friendly outgoing individual who enjoys and adds to the communal aspect of the sport.

"What all do you do?" I ask him.

In a rhythmic chant he reels off, "I do horse shows, rodeos, Hillbilly Barn Dances, goat tieings, wakes and weddings, the odd bar mitzva, commercials, Queen Contests, team ropings, but I don't do auctions." Then he adds, "I leave that to Jack Daines."

I want to get together with Bill for a longer chat, but his schedule was extremely busy and we weren't able to find a convenient time. We thought we would get together in Vancouver, but that didn't happen either.

Jack sits with me on the bench in front of the rodeo office while cowboys wander to and fro. They stand in small groups chatting before going over to the grandstand.

"Saddle bronc riding has run deep in our blood for generations, but I have to tip my hat to the bull riders for the great success they have had with their event," Jack states. "And I like watching them." He sits close, talking confidentially, as if this is the most important thing he can be doing at the moment.

"The rules of bull riding are simple, stay on 'til the end and don't slap the bull with your free hand. There are more technicalities in other sports, but there isn't more excitement. I quit the sport when I was 21 and it was a very exciting lifestyle, which I greatly missed.

"Bull riders are a breed of their own," he continues. "In no other sport do they have to put their life on the line, outmatched 10 to 1 in size, 150 lbs to 1500-1800 lbs for their opponent. In no other sport do they pay an entry fee to compete against their best friends to win. They have no team coach, they have no travel director and no team manager. They make their own hotel reservations and their own travel reservations. They pick the rodeos they want to go to, and when you add it all up, the sport of Pro Rodeo, featuring bull riding, makes all other sports look like games."

Like other sports, bull riding has seen its changes, with bulls and riders constantly improving. "Now, the bulls are 40 times ranker than what they used to be. Gerdy and Tiger, they were two outstanding bulls in their time. Now they'd be just two more bulls in the field. At Ponoka there were no qualifiers in the final round of the bull riding. The rankness of the bull has increased that much that on almost every ride the cowboy knows he's getting a bull that's going to give him a hell of a trip." Jack punctuates his ideas with his voice.

"Bodacious is a prime example of how rank the bulls have gotten. They finally pulled him out, retired him, which was the first time in history they pulled a bull because he was so rank."

Cowboys walking by say hello to Jack. The numbers are growing, as is the interest and electricity in the air as they anticipate the final day of the World Famous Calgary Stampede. "Like in all sports," Jack continues, "the cowboys are training better and sports medicine has improved tremendously. Also, they can watch videos of all the bulls. Before you barely got a good picture of a bull, so you wouldn't know what you were getting on. The guys would tell you if it was good or not so good, but today the bull riders can study the bull they're going to be getting on. You can watch him 100 times before you get on him."

Jack carries a lot of sincerity in his voice and his long experience in the business ensures people trust and respect him. When he says, "Bull Riding is the only event in rodeo that can stand on its feet without other rodeo events," you can believe him. And like the riders themselves, he believes, "they don't get a fair cut of the money."

"In other rodeo events they start when they are 18 and they can go until they're 40. Bull riders, by the time they are 22-23, their careers are over. There are a few exceptions, but not many. All indications are that many of the people in the crowd come out just to see the bull riders. Bull riding packs a lot of weight. Fans are more knowledgeable, as is the media."

Jack points out that the corporate sponsors, Wrangler, Dodge, Molson's, Budwiser and Dewalts, "just to mention a few" have also made a significant contribution to rodeo by putting a lot of money into the sport.

Sitting on the benches that are part of the history of the Calgary Stampede puts Jack in a reflective mood, "I came down here on the train in 1945; I was nine years old. The rodeo mesmerized me and I was hooked. Calgary is the biggest show. You make sure you put that in there. For the people who love rodeo it is their Stanley Cup, World Series, Christmas and Easter all rolled into one. They wait all year for the Stampede."

Like many ranchers and cowboys, Jack Daines has experienced first hand the dangers of the rodeo. His son, Duane, a Saddle Bronc rider, was seriously injured in the arena. Jack speaks of him with pride. "He went to the NFR nine times, he was a $50 000 winner at Calgary, he was High School All Round Champion for Canada and was three times the Canadian All Round Champion. The highlight of his career was when he was named Cowboy of the Year in 1995.

"Now he is in a wheel chair for life, and making a big contribution to where the sport is heading," Jack points out. Duane is on the Board of Directors of the CPRA.

Whatever the Daines suffered with Duane's accident, whatever they went through during the time of his recovery, there was no hint of self pity in Jack's voice, words or attitude. He embodied the attitude of so many of the ranchers and rodeo participants, whatever has gone before is done, and now there is only going forward.

He has work to do, so I wander around and chat with a few others. That morning, before I came to the grounds, I had been looking at pictures I had taken at Williams Lake, and had a good one of Jim Leatherberry.

I saw Jim talking with someone so went over to say hello, and much to my surprise he replies, "I'm not Leatherberry," he laughs. "I often get mistaken for him. One time a photographer came up to me and said, 'I got a good picture of you riding a bull.' 'No you don't,' I told him. 'I don't ride bulls.'"

The small tractors with passenger trailers shuttle people into the grounds and the crowds outside the Rodeo Office begin to thin as two o'clock approaches when the events will get underway.

I sit down on one of the benches, once again feeling left out, alone and discouraged at not being able to get in the arena where I can talk more with the cowboys, get more of the color and more of their stories. There is no point buying a ticket to the grandstand, as I'd see less there than what I'd be able to see on TV.

I say hello to the fellow sitting next to me, who is waiting for a friend to show up. Gordon Fenton, from Irma, Alberta, is no longer rodeoing, but is involved with cattle; buying and selling. "I work for different auction marts, getting customers to bring cattle to auction," he tells me.

The 27-year-old hadn't been a contestant for five years, and though bull riding wasn't his main sport, he did spend time on them.

"I got a scholarship to the College of South Idaho at Twin Falls. I roped calves, steer wrestled, team roped and rode bulls." In the classroom he took Liberal Arts, which included agricultural courses, "some stuff I could use, but other courses I was already educated in. Probably the courses that helped me the most were the computer classes."

Gordon has mixed feelings about the bulls. "I never wanted to make a career of it. We raised pure bred heifers and I know bulls. Riding them was not something I wanted to do. It was more fun roping and bulldogging."

But he did ride them and says it "was fun" until an injury put him out. "I rode 50-60 times before I got hurt. I broke a spur strap and was jerked down on the horn and broke two ribs, my breast bone and separated my shoulder. I spent three hours in the hospital. They gave me a Tylenol and sent me on my way. I flew home to Calgary and went to the Foothills Hospital and checked in. It never healed up right and it took me about two years to get over it."

"You remember your first ride?"

"I don't remember anything about it. The guys said I was making a hell of a ride but I don't know. I don't remember a thing about it."

"Was the travelling hard?"

"No, I didn't mind the travelling, but I don't like driving. I grew up always on the road. I can sleep anywhere. The night life is what the real problem is. Guys can get carried away with all them girls, they all like to chase you, and the guys like to chase them when you're young. It takes a pretty special girl to put up with a cowboy."

Gordon's friend doesn't show, and it is only a few minutes before the events are to begin, so he offers to take me in as his guest.

I am elated, as there is nothing like being down on the ground, mingling with the cowboys, their friends and their family. Being in the dust, with the smell of the animals, the noise and having the opportunity to talk with the people. Though Calgary is not like Williams Lake, where I had access to the riders before and after they competed, it is still a good place to be. It is exciting and often I get caught up in the moment and forget to take notes of what is happening. Sometimes I jot things down that I didn't put in context, and later they made no sense:

hear you, kick your butt

60 Minutes – 2 hours

Taco Bell – Mexican Telephone company

Shelly A. is here, "Chad's going to ride in Nanton tonight. Are you going to go down?"

"Yeah, I probably will. I've got my car if anyone would like a ride."

Bull and rider go in different directions at the Calgary Stampede.

Tammy, with her usual amount of lipstick and make-up, the tight jeans and halter top, is a little out of sorts, "Robert is down in the States and he's missed his plane. I don't know if he'll make it back on time to ride."

He didn't.

It is a tough afternoon on Canadian bull riders. Glenn Keeley – bucked off. Quinton Lowery – bucked off. Quinn Franklin – bucked off. Kelly Armstrong, leading the Canadian standings, doesn't add to his points – bucked off.

Tuff Hedeman has the best ride of the day, getting an 85.5 from the judges. Josh O'Byrne sticks to Tremors for second place and a shot at the $50 000 on Sunday, but it is Jim Hart who claims the Calgary aggregate title with a 79.5 ride. It is fourth best for the afternoon, but enough to win Calgary. Only four of the 12 semi-finalists rode for the full eight seconds. Hart's three rides totalled 242 points. It wasn't a particularly pretty ride on Bruce Sunstrum's Glory Days, a bull he didn't particularly want to ride. He was strung out on the bull for most of the trip but through grit and determination he held on to the end, and the title.

Jim Sharp, an early leader, got bucked and then his bull went rank and gave bullfighter Mike Matt a rough ride, which ended by Mike being tossed heavily against the fence off the horns of the bull. Mike worked that night down in Nanton.

When Tragedy Hits ...

During the intermission I go to the concession and buy a roast beef sandwich. It's soggy and tasteless and undoubtedly the worst sandwich I've eaten in a long time. It messes with my innards when I return to the arena to watch the second half of the program.

The humor of Lecile Harris, Rodeo Clown of the Year, keeps the crowd chuckling: "You think my name is funny, but it's not as funny as my brother's," he says in that southern drawl that all the clowns affect. "My dad's name is Ferdinand, my mother's name is Lisa – they named my brother Ferdalizer."

One of the differences at today's events is that the winners are brought up on stage, lead there on the arm of a beautiful girl. It is a great thrill for the cowboys to be up in front of the large crowd. Hart, in addition to winning the $8900 prize money, is presented with a diamond ring and a $1000 bonus from Justin Boots. Some of that sponsorship money that Jack Daines referred to.

When the events are over the cowboys, friends and family are in no rush to leave. They crowd into the beer gardens, take all the seats at all the tables and stand about in groups. I buy a much-needed beer, then say hello to Austin Beasley.

"I'm sorry I didn't call you," he says. "But I didn't go to Wyoming. I got headed by the bull and my back was pretty sore. I couldn't see myself driving for 12 hours."

"Yeah, I saw that on TV. Thought you might not feel like going too far after that."

Austin introduces me to Johnny Gann, a bareback rider from north central Texas who arrived in Canada the day before. The short and stocky Gann is about as good natured a fellow as you'd hope to meet. I'd be hard put to say who smiles the most, Johnny or Jay Manning.

Austin has his wallet in hand, getting money for beer, then he tucks it inside his cowboy boot. He goes off for the beer and I talk with Johnny. They are planning to go to Nanton, even though Austin isn't riding. He's going to help around the chutes. They've got room in their pick-up, so I arrange to go with them.

When Austin returns, he introduces me to his mother and I spend a lot of time talking with her.

"You should write about the Cowboys' Benefit Fund," she tells me.

"What's that?"

"In 1989 four cowboys were going down to the States to ride in the rodeo. Their plane crashed in the mountains and killed all of them, Brian Claypool, Calvin Bunney, Lee Coleman and Gary Logan. What made it worse is that they didn't find the plane for several months. There was a huge search and rescue operation and people from all over were sending money to help out. It was really a tough time for rodeo people, we all feel like family, and when tragedy hits one, it hits us all."

A small group of her friends are clustered together and they confirm what she is saying by nodding, agreeing and adding their two bits.

"Over $200 000 was raised for the search, but when they were eventually found there was still a lot of money left over. What they did was they had some bronze sculptures made, but the families felt that the money should have gone to helping other cowboys and their families who are in need. So what they did was set up the Cowboys' Benefit Fund. That's been going since 1980.

"Every year at the Canadian Finals Rodeo in Edmonton a Fashion Show and Luncheon are held to raise funds for the Benefit. This year there's going to be a special tribute to the mothers of the deceased cowboys. You should write about it," she encourages me. "It's going to be really good. Are you going to make it to the CFR?"

"I really don't know," I answer. "I'd like to get to Edmonton for it, but I don't know if I'll be able to."

"You really should come."

I nod. Thinking about this tragedy, I say, "It must be very hard on mothers to see their sons go off to the rodeo, especially when they start so young."

"You worry a lot," she says and two of her friends, also mothers of rodeo competitors, chime in, in agreement. And there is no argument when Mrs. Beasley adds, "But you can't stop them. If it is something they have to do then they have to do it. If it is in their system, then that is what they are going to do. I would never encourage a child of mine to get into it, but there is nothing I would do to keep them out."

The sun is relentless, slowly cooking me, so I baste my innards with another beer while I wait for Austin to make his move. Cowboys seem to like waiting for the last moment before leaving. It's over an hour's drive down to Nanton but we don't leave until 6:30 for the 7:30 start.

"Will you be here tomorrow?" Mrs. Beasely asks.

"I don't think so," I reply, explaining my problems with getting into the grounds.

No one is surprised. "All the families have the same problem," one of the friends says in an acid tone. "Calgary is only interested in money. The cowboys and their families make the Stampede, but they do as little in return as they can for them."

I'm getting a little anxious to leave, so I excuse myself and look for Austin and Johnny. I find Johnny. "What's Austin up to?"

"I think he's trying to talk that blonde into going with us."

Indeed he was, and he is successful in his efforts.

They stride over and he introduces us to Kerri Aaskow, Shelly's younger, but taller, sister. We walk through the parking lot to Austin's pick-up, which the four of us squeeze into. Kerri is next to Austin and Johnny next to her, and I'm against the door.

"Did you see that Tammy girl?" Johnny asks as we spin out of the parking lot.

"The one that wears so much make-up?"

"Yeah."

"She wears her lipstick up over her nose," Austin pouts his lips and draws an imaginary line up over his nose.

"That's the one."

"At least it covers her moustache."

"The girl who was wearing the halter top and the tight pants?" I ask, making sure I wasn't confusing her with someone else. Just as there is more than one Shelly, there is more than one Tammy.

"That's the one," Kerri says.

"She is the most annoying person in the world," is Austin's opinion, which gets us laughing.

"Tell him the story," Kerri urges.

Austin doesn't want to. He's busy passing every vehicle on the road and weaving through traffic to pass those that won't get out of the way.

I try to encourage him, but his reluctance to talk is difficult to overcome. Finally he relents, "I'll tell you this story," he says. "I was coming back from Texas alone. I was going through California when I see Robert Bowers and this Tammy girl hitch-hiking. I give them a ride and two minutes after they get into the truck, I want to throw her out. And we had a 15-hour drive ahead of us. She is the most annoying person in the world that I've ever met. Everything 'amazed' her and she talked and talked and she wouldn't shut up. I was ready to jump out of the truck and take my own life. There was nothing you could do to shut her up. I cranked the radio up and tried to listen to it. But she kept going on and on. She had a real hard time being quiet. She was driving me bonkers.

"Finally we get to Golden, it's late at night and I tell her and Robert to go in the back and get some sleep. She doesn't want to go. 'We're all right,' she says. 'No you're not. Get in the back!' Austin's voice is strained. "I finally convinced them to get in the back and I drove the rest of the way to Calgary without stopping. I wasn't going to give her a chance to get back in the cab. I rode slack the next morning at 8:30."

"Is she going with Robert?" I ask.

"She'd like to."

"I talked to her, and she made a big point that she was just friends with him."

We hit the Number 2 highway, and get in the fast lane, where Austin bullies everyone into getting out of our way. He comes right up on their tail and stays there until they move. Some get out of the way a little quicker than others, but one car just doesn't seem to get the idea that he is in the way and he should find somewhere else to drive.

Johnny, Kerri and I do most of the talking while Austin drives. Tammy is a topic Austin is familiar with, having been Bower's roommate when they were in college in the States.

"Robert would tell me that if that Tammy girl phones to tell her I'm not in," Austin looks over at us as he talks. Checks the road, "So she would phone and I would answer it and say, 'Is this Tammy?' 'Yes.' 'Just a minute, he's right here.' When Robert wasn't in I'd say, 'Just a minute.' I would wait, then come back on the phone and pretend to be Robert. She wouldn't know the difference. She'd say, 'Why didn't you come to see me when you were up? You promised me you were going to.' I'd answer, 'I meant to, but I was really busy and I just couldn't make it. I really wanted to see you. I promise you the next time I come up I'll call you.'"

Of course he wouldn't tell Robert any of this, and so on his next trip Robert wouldn't call Tammy and Tammy would call back and give him hell for not seeing her when he promised he would.

Kerri reacts with surprise, "She told me she was always getting mixed messages from Robert."

Little wonder, when one time she is talking with Robert and the next time with Austin.

At Nanton they charge us $24 to get in. Austin and one guest are allowed in free, but two of us have to pay. Austin pays for the tickets, even though I insist on paying for myself. He'd hear nothing of it, so I promised to get the beer.

They Can't Be Tamed

The rodeo grounds on the outskirts of Nanton sit on a slight rise not too distant from the highway, just out of town. Behind the chutes, the prairie stretches away to the northwest and the foothills of the Rocky Mountains. It is not as flat here as out at Cereal, but it has that same small town intimacy. I am able to get behind the chutes and mingle with the contestants, the people helping out, and friends and family.

Every cowboy has a kit bag full of tape.

Glen Keeley walks by. His face has been scraped up since the last time I've seen him. He's from Nanton and down here they are proud of the young man who was the Canadian Champion in 1989.

"Hey Floyd," Jay Manning calls to me, "You made it down."

"How's it going?"

Jay is smiling, but he appears to have less energy than usual.

"You going to be at Calgary tomorrow?" he asks.

"I don't know. I have a hell of a time getting in."

"It's a glorified Jackpot. I've always gotta do backflips to get in."

We chat for a while before he goes off to prepare for his ride.

Clint comes by and slaps me on the chest. He's ready to ride. "Hey Matty," he says to another rider, "Why do you tape up both your hands?"

"That's 'cause when I get on him, I look to see if he's got a twinkle in his eye so I know which way he's going to turn," he moves his hands as if he's switching them on the rope.

Clint is sceptical.

"Naw, I've got a broken bone in my free hand."

"Good evening, ladies and gentlemen," announcer Joe Bradlock welcomes the audience to "two and a half hours in the wild west."

The wind drags the cutting, arid air through a twilight that lingers long into the evening. The slanting sun slips yellowing rays through the gaps in the fences and chutes carrying shadows further and further into the arena as the wild west show goes on.

The bulls seem particularly rank this evening. They are banging about in the chutes, bellowing and protesting and not co-operating in any manner whatsoever. The atmosphere here is so different from Calgary. This is not so much a show, but a contest. A dangerous contest without the big prizes, without the publicity, with a handful of people watching, in contrast to the thousands at Calgary. Not to give the impression that it isn't a good turnout. It's an excellent turnout, a family event, and a community gathering where everyone knows everyone else.

I'm surprised to see Chad Wakefield taped up, wearing a flack jacket under his vest and ready to ride.

"I thought you were retired," I say to him.

"I thought I'd give it a try. Just to see how I do."

Unfortunately he doesn't make the eight seconds and the disappointment shows as he walks out of the arena, head down. But he hasn't ridden for a long time and he expected to be a little rusty.

I wander back and forth behind the chutes and a lot of the riders recognize me. I almost feel a part of the group. I nod to Rick Henderson and he nods back, but later comes over and says, "Sorry I didn't talk to you earlier. I met you in Williams Lake," he apologizes for not being friendlier, but I don't expect anything more. They have work to do and I'm not expecting them to be social, though Jay and Clint certainly are. And Johnny grins and we chat when we find ourselves next to each other watching a ride.

During the first half of the bull-o-rama, I stand near the gate where two St Johns Ambulance people are on the ready with a stretcher and the ambulance parked nearby. One medic, a young lady, has attended a lot of these rodeos in a professional capacity. But she says she doesn't like them. She laughs a lot and asks me what I'm doing. Fortunately, during this go round she has no more to do than to stand and watch the cowboys hit the dust.

"If you don't like your children, you let them stand along the fence," Joe Bradlock tells the audience. There are a number of youngsters playing near the fence and their parents call to them to get back.

When I went to Luxton I found myself keeping a good distance from the bulls, but the more time I spend down by the chutes the less nervous I feel. I find I can stand and take a picture of a bull charging straight at me without backing up, and keeping my mind on what I'm doing. A certain confidence in the fencing is required.

When an energetic bull tosses his rider, then turns and looks in my direction, I feel no reason to move. But there's a 10-year-old boy standing in front of me and when he sees the bull heading in his direction he turns and bolts faster than a jack rabbit. Unfortunately, I'm standing in his way, which hinders his retreat, but only briefly.

Jay has a hell of time with his bull. It kicks and bucks and bangs about in the chute and it is a long time before they can open the gate to let him out. Just as the gate opens Jay gets on him, and it is only a few moments more and he is off. Jay isn't smiling when he comes out of the arena. He is in the most serious mood I've seen him in. Serious, but not glum.

The long evening lingers like a leaf drifting earthward, but when the riding is over there is a dance to be enjoyed in the Quonset building. I don't wait for the others to tag along. It's now 9:30 and I need to eat something to rid myself of the memory of that sandwich I had in Calgary. I don't feel great. These long days are going to kill me.

Smokies are the most appetizing of the food on sale, so I buy one and wolf it down before Austin, Kerri and Johnny join the growing crowd. The band is at the opposite end of the building and people don't wait much before they begin to dance. The floor is a thick carpet of gravel which crunches underfoot. A low maintenance floor.

I buy the first round of drinks.

Shelly and Chad join the group and we all chat and chatter and drink and they go off to get some food.

Kerri says to Austin, "Tell him about Chad and the Ferris Wheel girl."

"No, I don't think Chad'd want that in the book."

I figure it must be something I'd want in the book.

"He was in a Ferris Wheel with Tammy . . ." Kerri begins.

"The same Tammy?"

"No! Not that one. A different one."

"This Tammy was about 16 years old," Austin interjects. "They were getting it on in the Ferris Wheel at the fair that was near the rodeo grounds. The security guards came and started poking around; I guess they knew that somebody had gotten in there, but they didn't see who it was. Chad and Tammy panic and they're getting themselves together and they fall out of the Ferris Wheel and they start to run. The security guards come chasing after them, but they managed to outrun them."

People drift around and the three of them go off to talk to others and I fall into conversation with Danny Thomson of Black Diamond. The 26-year-old has been riding bulls since he was 16 and was on the steers before that. "My Dad boxes, but my grandfather was a champion on the bulls," he says.

Checking the stats I found two Thomsons listed. Harry, who won the bull riding championship in 1946 and again in '49, and Ralph, who was the 1947 champion.

"The first 50 to 100 bulls you ride, it's all a blur," he says. "But you've got to get the basics down and gear your mind to it. If you think about it too much you're going to get bucked off."

"What's it like to get bucked off?"

"Sometimes I get bucked off and I never know if I'm going to land. There is all that air before you hit. But there is nothing to compare with bull riding. Sure you hurt and financially it wasn't so good, but there is nothing else like it. I guess what I found the toughest was all the travelling."

I am beginning to understand that first hand.

Kerri comes back. She tells me she started competitively in rodeo when she was 10 years old. She does barrel racing and team roping. "In High School Rodeo I did a lot of events," she sips on a Coors.

"Is it true that girls are attracted to the bull riders?"

She nods, "In high school they were. Whatever they thought about them they were in for a shock."

"Why were they so interested in them?"

"I think it was because they wanted to tame them. The bull riders are the bad asses. They were the ones that were always drinking and trying not to get caught. They're the guys that do all the wild sports and the girls think 'I'm going to make him mine and he's going to do what I want. I'm going to tame him.' But like I said, they are in for a shock, because they're not going to tame them."

"How long have you known Austin?"

"About a year."

"Are you going with him?"

"I was 'in lust' with him. But he said I was too young. He wanted someone he could go to the bar with."

"How old are you?"

"I'm 18."

When Austin joins us, I buy some more drinks and everybody stands around smiling at each other.

"Tell him about . . ." Kerri leans close to Austin and I can't hear what she's saying.

He shakes his head.

"Tell him about . . ."

"No!" Austin responds.

So we drink our beer and I relax for a moment. Still feeling rough.

"Okay," Austin says, "Here's a story I can tell you." He takes a step closer and thinks about how to begin. "Day One." He stops, then starts again. "I went south for the winter rodeo with Kelly Armstrong and we went down to Vernon, Texas, where Mike White was staying. This was the first time I met him. I didn't know him, but as we went to the rodeos he seemed like a pretty good guy. He was riding like a demon, he was phenomenal. Everything was going fine until the spring and we decided to go out to California. We were staying in Texas. We went to Red Bluff and then we were going to two different rodeos. I had a short run at Red Bluff then I caught a ride to the other rodeo.

"When that was finished, I was to call him on his cell phone and he was going to pick me up. So I called, but I couldn't get him. So I hang around and wait. It's now about 7:30 and he's still not there, so I go for a beer and hang around and wait with some people and I try and get him again, but still no answer. Finally these people say that I can go with them and they give me a ride. I didn't know any of them. I keep trying to phone him, but I never get him. So I'm stuck with these people I don't know and I stay the night with them.

"Finally I get a hold of him the next morning and he's in Flagstaff, Arizona. He says to me, 'I drove by and didn't see you, so I thought you were coming with someone else.' 'Why would I be going with someone else when all my stuff is in your truck?' I tell him. 'I've spent the last 22 hours with only my rigging bag.' I'm really pissed at him.

"'Sorry,' was all he said and I've got to get myself home. He deliberately turned off his phone so that he wouldn't have to pick me up. I was really pissed off.

"So I get a ride with these three people and they've got these saddles all stacked up in the back seat and I'm stuck in between them all and I couldn't move. It was like you're in a coffin. We drove for 14 or 15 hours like this to Albuquerque, New Mexico. Fourteen to 15 hours sitting like that, without being able to move. Then, in Albuquerque I had to hitchhike. They left me at a truck stop and told me I'd be able to get a ride with one of the truckers, no problem. So I talk to the truckers. 'Are you going east?' I ask. 'Nope.' 'You going east?' 'No.' Then they tell me that they can't give me a ride because the trucking company won't let them carry extra riders.

"So I went out on the road and hitchhiked and had to wait for five hours before I got a ride. Five hours standing at the side of the road and nobody would stop. Finally I get a ride. A half an hour into the ride he asks me if I'll drive, so I drove from 2:00 a.m. until 6:00 and I didn't get any sleep at all that night.

"The next ride I get in and I'm out like a light. I'm so tired I could've slept on a rock. Suddenly he's shaking me saying, 'Hey! Hey! You've got to get out. This is where we turn off.'

"I'm still asleep and I stumble out and I'm in this flat ass country and the wind is blowing 800 miles an hour and there is nothing there. The first truck goes roaring by and my hat goes flying 20 feet into the ditch."

"How much did you pay for that hat?" I ask.

"$285."

He continues, "I'm out there for an hour and a half and nobody stops and for an hour and a half I'm cursing fucking Mike White, you son-of-a-bitch! Then some goofball picks me up. 'I'll get you to Amarillo,' he says. He's a weirdo. 'Do you do drugs?' he asks me. 'No, no.' I say to him but for 100 miles he never once stops talking about the evils of drugs. When we get to Amarillo, it's raining, raining hard, but I'm glad to get out of his car. But then I get soaked and all the cars going by are spraying me and I'm really pissed off. Finally a trucker stops and picks me up and drops me near Kelly's house, my girlfriend at the time. I walked over there, but she wasn't home. Shelly's there and she opens the door to this guy who is beat-up, greasy, dirty, smelly and stinking, and my armpits are reeking, my breath is horrible. I haven't brushed my teeth in days, I haven't showered, I haven't changed my clothes. I'm a real mess.

"Shelly says, 'What the hell were you doing?' She gave me a ride home."

"That sounds like the incredible journey."

Austin has stopped talking, but the story is not yet over. "The next week we're flying around to four rodeos. I get on the plane and I take my seat and who's sitting next to me? Mike White. I'm stuck there next to him for 10 hours and we don't say a word to each other the entire time. I could still kill him. I called him all night and I kept thinking, 'Surely to God, he'll turn his phone on.'" Austin shakes his head. He still can't believe that Mike White didn't turn his phone on.

Kerri is smiling. Johnny drinks his beer.

"He just wanted to see his girl. We weren't entered in any rodeos, so it wasn't like he had to get somewhere."

The Legends

"Dhum Dhum Dhum Dhum . . ." the music pounds throughout the cab of Austin's Dodge pick-up as the headlights cut a narrow path through the black night, lighting up the highway. Off the highway, scattered in the distance, are tiny jewels of light from small towns, while ahead the massive urban sprawl of Calgary gives a silver glow to the sky, dimming all the stars in the heavens.

We left the dance at Nanton at 11:00, stopped at a service station to service ourselves, as well as gas up and then head north to the city. I still feel miserable. I'm exhausted and the food I'd eaten didn't sustain me for very long. It has been a long draining day, and it is far from over.

On the highway Austin cranks up the music, Kerri eats from a carton of instant soup and the smile still hasn't left Johnny's face.

"Dhum Dhum Dhum Dhum . . ."

"This should be the song they play before the bull riding starts," I suggest.

Austin gives me a look. I don't think he agrees. Kerri is puzzled until the words start, "Dhum Dhum Dhum Dhum . . . Another one bites the dust! And another one goes and another one goes . . ."

Kerri finishes about half the soup and asks me to throw it out, but I'm still hungry, so I polish it off in short order and it makes me feel much better.

I become more talkative, even though I should realize that when Austin cranks up the music, it means he wants to drive and not talk. There is still a lot I want to know. To get things started I ask Austin which bull riders he likes.

"Jim Sharp, Tuff Hedeman and Clint Branger, he's going to be really good."

"What makes them good?"

"Staying on the bull all the time," he answers.

I think that would do it, but what I want to know is why some riders are able to stay on longer than others.

"Some guys try harder."

"Do they have better co-ordination?"

"I don't think so. You watch Tuff. He's totally unco-ordinated. He's clumsier than shit but he just kept trying. He never gave up. He has a heart the size of a truck."

"What did you think of the movie *Eight Seconds*?"

"Not much."

Few bull riders do like the movie. One comment was that it made Lane Frost and Tuff Hedeman look like a couple of nobodies who suddenly start riding well, rather than the professionals they are/were, who developed their skills over years of riding. Some didn't like the fact that it delved into Lane's personal life and dug up a lot of dirt.

One element that was wrong was the impression they gave that Tuff Hedeman was just an average cowboy following along in the wake of the great Lane Frost. The movie would lead you to believe that it wasn't until a bull put a horn into Lane's ribs, puncturing his heart, that Tuff suddenly got his act together and started riding like a wolf.

The statistics show a different story. In 1984 Tuff Hedeman is listed in 12th place in the All-Around Cowboy standings. Lane Frost is not listed. In the Bull Riding standings Lane is 9th while Tuff is 10th. In 1985 Tuff climbed to 7th in All Around, was 2nd in Bull Riding, earning $102 328, substantially ahead of Frost's 3rd place finish with earnings of $87 100. In 1986 Tuff was 3rd in the All-Around standings and 1st in the Bull Riding with record earnings of $137 061 (a mark surpassed only once in the following 10 years) with Lane Frost still in 3rd place, but with $104 128 winnings in his pockets.

In 1987 Tuff slipped to 6th place in the All-Around Cowboy earnings and he traded places with Lane, who took the top spot as he fell to third in the Bull Riding. Interestingly enough, Frost's earnings were only slightly more than the previous year $105 697, certainly nothing to sneeze at, while Hedeman's earnings had dropped to $98 129.

In 1988 Hedeman again was 6th in the All-Around Cowboy standings and was 3rd in Bull Riding, while Frost slipped to 6th place. Frost was killed in July 1989 at the Cheyenne Frontier Days Rodeo by a bull named Taking Care of Business. That year Hedeman won the Championship with $122 765 in earnings and has remained in the top 10 every year except 1994.

This is not to diminish in any way what Frost did in the arena, nor the type of person he was. When Frost died the rodeo world lost a great star and one who did a lot to improve the image of the sport. He was a great bull rider and one who earned the adulation of his many admirers.

Although Taking Care of Business ended Frost's life, it is another bull, the famous Red Rock, that is more often thought of when Frost's name is raised. When Frost met the unridden Red Rock in a seven match series in 1988, the cowboy beat the bull 4-3. Before that, Red Rock had thrown 309 consecutive riders.

I think it's only appropriate that Tuff Hedeman have the last say, here, about his good friend and travelling partner. He's been quoted as saying: "We were the last ones to leave no matter where we were at. If there was somebody who came to say 'hi' to him, he'd always find the time, if we had somewhere we needed to be or not – no matter how big or small, young or old, rich or poor. I never introduced him to anyone who didn't think he was the greatest. He just had a magic to him. He left everybody with a smile."

But make no mistake, Tuff Hedeman is an outstanding athlete in his own right.

Good bulls buck most guys off. Great Bulls buck everybody off.

Wayne Vold
Stock Contractor

Suicide Sirloin

In recent years bulls have gotten ranker, quicker and smarter. They are half the rodeo event, and though the fans don't pay them as much attention as they should, the riders and the stock contractors certainly do. Without rank bulls going out and doing their utmost to get rid of that pesky cowboy, there wouldn't be much of a show. Not only do the contractors and riders know the value of the bulls and respect them, many feel affection for them.

There is a great similarity between the cowboy and the bulls – other than looks. Like the cowboys the bulls are required to "go down the road," though their view of the road is different than the cowboy's, and they never have to get behind the donut and drive. The bulls are athletes who can have their off days, just like any other athlete. But they want to do their best, and as the cowboys get smarter with experience, so do the bulls. The tricks that fooled them as youngsters are scoffed at as they mature. The great bulls want to entertain the crowd, and so often they do.

There are bulls who go out, do their job, then head home to the wife and kids. Others like to party and be the centre of attention. They trot around the arena, strutting their stuff. Anyone who gets in their way is dealt with. It is their show and they are in charge. However, as occasionally happens with a cowboy, someone has to keep them in line. When a bull refuses to return to the pens, one or two bulls are released into the arena. They go out, butt heads, have a chat and trot back into the pens, followed by the recalcitrant bull.

Bulls are as individual and different as people. Some have become legends. The rankest of them all was Bodacious, the only bull that had to be retired because he was too mean. He smashed Tuff Hedeman's face for him and Tuff promised his son never to ride him again. Then there was Red

Rock that year after year tossed cowboys until age and Lane Frost caught up with him. Even the greats get old, if they live long enough.

Most bulls have a career of "six to seven years, while the odd one makes it to ten years," according to Earl Call of C + Rodeo Company, located 15 miles south of Williams Lake on the Horsefly Road.

Over the years bulls have been bred to the life of the arena. When the sport started it was called Brahma Bull riding. The Brahmas were big and not particularly mean.

Earl explains what happened, "The Brahmas were brought up here for the rodeo, but there were some problems with them. They don't winter very well and they don't travel well. The Brahmas are about 2000 pounds, which makes travelling very hard on them. It is hard on their legs. The smaller ones (1500-1600 lbs.) haul a lot better. A five or six hour trip is no big deal for them."

Earl says that ideal bulls are "a cross that have speed, quickness and fight, and they can take the winters. Their ideal weight is between 1500-1600 lbs. while the young ones are 1400 lbs. They fill out as they get older."

The Brahmas were crossed with herd bulls, Black Angus, Charolais and the like. "When we are looking at a young bull to decide if he'd be good for the rodeo, we look at his temperament. Do they want to fight? Do they want to hook someone? When they are young they don't have to buck, but if they like to hook, we'll keep them."

The stockyards at the Luxton Pro Rodeo.

The stock contractors do not only consider the bull in their breeding program, they will also test the heifers to see how well they buck. It is a 50/50 proposition, with half the temperament of the offspring coming from the cow and half from the bull.

Earl and his brother Roy have been doing rodeo for about 10 years, providing stock for rodeos in Western Canada. "We go as far north as Grande Prairie and south to Victoria, to the Luxton Rodeo. We don't go to the States, it's not worth the problems," Earl told me one morning at Williams Lake. He was dressed in a t-shirt and looked as muscular and healthy as the bulls he provides the stampedes with.

C+ Rodeo, which was established in 1983, has about 55 bulls, but those numbers will change over the course of a year. They like to keep the numbers down during the winter when they are not productive and have to be fed and cared for.

The question of whether the bulls are being treated well is only one that concerns those who are not involved with the rodeo, or ranching.

"The animal rights guys are dwindling off," Earl states. "The truth of the matter is that if the bulls were not here they would be dead. I know that is kind of blunt, but that is the reality. There would be no use for a bull with odd colors, or if he's too mean. Some people might not like that, but that's the way it is. The crowd likes the bull riding, and the bulls have a good life. They only work about ten minutes a year."

Wayne Vold agrees, "They have an easy life," he says about rodeo bulls. "They work for eight seconds at a time, three months a year. If they buck good," he smiles "we let them out in the pasture and they can have half a dozen heifers. How tough can that be?"

At Calgary I sat in the beer garden in blazing sunshine, drinking beer and listening to Wayne, who has "been in the business all my life. My father started it 40 years ago." They have produced some excellent bulls, such as Bunny, Hagar, Rambo and Sugar Ray. Bunny and Hagar have been responsible for a lot of offspring. "They influenced a lot of good bulls," Wayne states.

"Bulls first came from India, then we got a few from Mexico in our breeding program. We wanted to get that hot blood."

Rambo was their first great bull. He was a little 1300 lb. bull who "bucked off a lot of good ones." He was always amongst the top rated bulls. From him came Bunny, and one shouldn't be misled by that name. Bunny too was a great bucking bull that made it to the final 10. Sugar Ray was the third generation bull who won recognition at the rodeos. Curley Sue is now bucking in the arena, the fourth generation bull in that line.

"If they buck, and they buck good, you can tell people about them. If they buck real good then people will tell you about them. Good bulls buck most guys off. Great bulls buck everybody off."

Bruce Sunstrum was sharing the table and enjoying a beer on a hot afternoon. He explained how they decide which bull is going to the rodeo. "When you buck them they have to have the desire to buck, if they don't have it there isn't much you can do. Some of the ugliest ones are the best buckers and the better looking ones aren't so good."

Just like a cowboy, you can't tell how good a bull is just by looking at him. And just like cowboys there are days when they'd prefer to stay at home with the heifers. "I really like the bulls," Bruce says. "Other than the fact that they'll escape on you and wanna go with the cows and wreck the corrals and stuff, generally they're okay. They get used to it and they load into the trucks real good. They respect you and you respect them. They are fairly docile animals.

"People have the wrong impression of them," he continues. "They think they are mean and that they're killers, but they're not. They are athletes just like the cowboy. It is man against beast."

And like the bull riders their careers tend to be short. "By the time they are 10-12 they're done," Bruce takes a sip of beer. "Bulls age too soon. They'll have five or six years in the rodeo. They start when they are four years old and depending on injuries, they'll finish up when they're eight or nine.

Bull riding at the Williams Lake Stampede.

"Most of their injuries are leg injuries. They'll pull a muscle or get a sore foot. Some of them try so hard they injure themselves. They are their own worst enemies," Bruce adds. "They will fight each other. They have their own pecking order, they're just like a cowboy who goes into a bar thinking he's tough and wants to prove it. The bulls are the same way."

Short Circuit is one of Bruce's favorite bulls. "He's a pet," he says. "He's 12 years old and during his career he was only rode about 10 times, and he bucked about 200 times." Big Louie is another favorite. "I bought him at an auction. He wasn't ridden for three years. He was really rank. Everybody hated to draw him because he was so rank, and he was dangerous."

The bull riders have their own opinions about the bulls, but they're not that much different than the stock contractors who raise them.

The best bulls are ones that give a good trip. The bull is responsible for half the points the cowboy gets. The cowboy's technique gets him the other half of the 100 points. So it is crucial to get a top score to get a bull that is going to give it his all when the chute opens.

At Williams Lake a cowboy slapped a bull that was in the chutes.

"Hey, don't do that," a bull rider says to him. "He's mad enough already."

"That could make the difference between a 79 and an 80," the other counters.

Don Nahrgang likes a bull "that really kicks hard and turns back either way." Shane Mills likes "spinners. I watch them to see what they do. Some bulls do the same trip each time, but most don't. The bulls enjoy it as much as we do. You can see it when they buck you off and they go running around the arena with their head held high. They're pretty proud when they win."

What most cowboys like is a bull that bucks everyone off. The cowboy that finally rides him climbs in stature.

Without the stock, there would be no rodeo. Without the bulls there would be no bull riders. The cowboys know this, and they treat the bulls with all the respect they deserve.

T Texas Terry
Bullfighter

Dancing with the One Ton Tornado

T Texas Terry

Don't mistake them, although bullfighters and clowns dress much the same, their jobs are completely different. The clowns are there to make you laugh. They're there for a good time. The bullfighter's business is very serious. They are there to save lives. And they do. But they're there for a good time too – when it goes well.

It doesn't always go well.

They too live by the bull rider's creed, "It is not a question of if you are going to be hurt, but when and how much."

And don't confuse North American rodeo bullfighters with Spanish and Mexican bullfighters. They don't dress anything alike and a mean bull is the only thing their occupations have in common. The North American bullfighter does nothing to injure the bull, though they might damage his ego.

Physically the bull is unharmed and comes back to play another day. Spanish bulls have a much shorter, more decisive ending to their careers.

It is easy to confuse clowns and bullfighters at the rodeo because they sometimes do the same job, getting a cowboy out of harm's way. A typical, though not universal, career may start as a cowboy in one of the events. For one reason or another the cowboy retires from his sport but wants to remain a part of the rodeo, so he becomes a bullfighter. When the bullfighters get older they "work the barrel," where they don't have to run around the arena as much as the other bullfighter.

The Man in the Can isn't about to show his face with the bull ready to give him a shot.

The profession has developed in recent years to the point where young men are now training for the business. They go to school and study the art of bullfighting. They are put in the arena with the bulls and given the basics. Then they go out with an established bullfighter and work, unpaid, with him. As their skills improve they begin to look for jobs on their own. During the time they apprentice they are making contacts with the rodeo committees and the people in the business doing the hiring. A good bullfighter is worth every cent he is paid.

"They are our life line," says BJ Smith. "Most of them are ex-riders, so they know the bull and they know the riders."

Just as bull riders like certain bulls, they also like certain bullfighters. "Everybody's got their preference for bullfighters. There are a lot of good bullfighters, but they can make errors just like we do. They save a lot of lives and a lot of injuries. A lot more guys would die if we didn't have bullfighters."

With most of the Luxton Rodeo crowd gone home, the security people went off to do other things and I wandered around back of the chutes and the pens where I found T Texas Terry putting away his gear for the night. He'd stripped off his oversized overalls to reveal bright red tights. He still had on his make up; white circles around the eyes and mouth outlined in black, and stars and stripes shirt.

"I've been working it for years," he says in a soft Texan drawl which is as warm as a summer's breeze. He bolts up one of the wheels on his mobile, which he uses in his act – mostly to fall to pieces or be taken apart.

"I guess you've seen a lot of Canada and the United States."

"No, this is my first time working in Canada," he replies. "Shit it's pretty up here. I'm from Delrio, Texas. Down there it is all brush and cactus and rocks."

I ask him if he needs a hand with anything, but he's fine. He's done this all too many times. He walks away, putting something in its place.

"I got into being a clown the same time I started riding," he comes back and gives me undivided attention. "I went to the rodeo and entered the bareback event. They didn't have any clowns and one guy got killed," the Texas drawl is a little softer when he recalls this. "I said I'm not going to another rodeo where they don't have a clown. If they don't have one then I'm going to do it. The next time I went to the manager and said I would do it. They paid me five bucks."

"Did you have any training?"

"Naaww," he draws out the word, dispelling such a foolish idea. "You just get out there and do what you're supposed to do. They didn't want to pay the money. I wanted ta do it, so I'd go do it."

What "you're suppose to do" is draw the attention of the bull from the rider, who may not know seven ways from Sunday after being tossed.

Despite being chased all over the infield and being rocked in the barrel, Terry Bowen (his other name) says, "I've never been hurt. I've got plenty of bumps and bruises, but I've never been hurt." His idea of hurt differs greatly from most of humanity's. "I've been hit with the horns, but not by nothin' that did any damage. I've been hit in the head and in the eye."

Terry says he's been married "all my life to the same woman." And just after I ask him about her, a tall blonde wearing jeans and a coat, and a baseball cap wanders over. Elaine seems a little peeved that Terry is wasting his time gabbing when she's hungry and wants to get something to eat.

"Why don't you go over to the hospitality tent and see what they've got," Terry suggests.

But she doesn't. She lingers about and in a little while gets into the conversation. "I don't worry about him anymore," she shakes her head. "There was the one time when he got turned upside down in the barrel and couldn't get out. The bull had hit the barrel and he got turned around and his feet were in the air and his head was on the ground, but I didn't know that. When he didn't come out I thought, whoa, something's wrong here. The guys went in and turned him around," she laughs. "It was really kind of funny after it's all done."

Terry fills in details from his point of view, "When you're in the barrel you don't want to stick your head out, because the bull might be right in your face, so you wait until they tell you to come out.

"This time the guys weren't telling me shit because they were all on the fence and the bull was looking for something to eat.

"You can't go too far south in those barrels, you've got about this much room at the top," he holds his hands about a foot apart. "The worst part is having to get in that damn thing. Some of the bulls can get their horns in that deep."

Looking at the short barrel I'm amazed that he can curl up in there at all.

"He didn't hurt me, it just pissed me off more than anything, that I'm upside down in there and nobody was doing nothing to get me out."

"Why do you do it? Why do guys get on an animal that seems intent on killing them?"

"For the money. Some of these guys can make real good money. I get between $500 and $750 a performance, it depends on the size of the rodeo. An outstanding type of an act would get $1500, but here they couldn't afford that."

And like most others, he loves the bulls. "I love bucking bulls."

"How do you spell that?" I interject.

"The ones I like start with a 'b'. The ones I don't like start with an 'f'. The ones I like will buck real good. And some will play with you. They'll hit the barrel, that's for the crowd. Sure, some of them are mean, but others are as gentle as dogs. You can walk over and scratch them on the ear.

"You study the bulls, and you talk it up with the other guys. Most bulls have a trip. They go the same way every time. Some of them fight, some of them don't."

But where's the fear? Sitting in the crowd you can feel the danger these animals create, you feel your own fear when they come charging to the fence in front of you. What are the guys who are squeezing down in the chute on the bare back of these beasts thinking and feeling?

T Texas Terry thrills the crowd at the Luxton Pro Rodeo.

"What he ought to be thinking," Terry looks at his pal Walter T Youngblood, a dummy dressed in big overalls and flannel shirt. "Is how to keep his head on. To work with the bull. When you start getting scared, that's when you should stop getting in there. You don't even think about it. You go do it, and it's over with. You don't think about it unless something hurts when you come down."

He smiles beneath his make up, "Walter T Youngblood, he's mean. He's not afraid of any bulls. He's been hooked, stomped on and rolled over, but he just keeps going back in there."

He's all done packing up and I'm keeping him from getting a meal, but he continues to talk. I don't think a person could get much more relaxed then he is.

"It's a rare thing when a man gets killed in this sport. In fact I read more about people being killed in hockey and football than in the rodeo. In the last 10 years, I only know of two guys who got killed. Lane Frost got killed in 1988, I can't remember the other guy's name. It's rare you get a horn. The other boy got stepped on, on the head. But that's rare."

T Texas Terry's opinion about cowboys is the same as BJ Smith's. "It's a lot of help me and help you. They'd do anything to help the other fellow out, then they will go into the arena and try and beat each other. They're very competitive."

How long can these men keep going in this sport? T Texas Terry is 54 years old and still very agile. "I hope I can keep going a while longer. I don't see any reason why I can't. Rick Young is still going and he's in his 60s. I keep in fairly decent shape by lifting weights. But I haven't been doing much of that lately," he admits looking at Elaine, who knows the truth.

Rick Young won the Coors "Man in the Can" award as recently as 1994 and in 1991. This award goes to the professional barrelman who scores highest in five different categories as judged by the 12 Wrangler Bullfight Tour participants, announcers and top bull riders.

"Has it been a good life?"

"It's been a lot of fun," he lets out his breath. "I did it my way. Did what I wanted to do."

He gives me his business card which says, "BAD BULLS ARE MY BUSINESS."

I walk back towards the fair grounds. It's quiet. Everyone has packed up, cleaned up and gotten ready for the evening's parties. Over the speakers around the arena Glenn Campbell's Rhinestone Cowboy is playing.

When I was in Williams Lake behind the chutes, I had a lot of time to observe and talk to the clowns and bullfighters. I asked the cowboys about the bullfighters and what Jim Leatherberry said was typical, "Bullfighting is a really tough job. If it wasn't for them there'd be a lot more guys hurt."

Every bull rider that I asked expressed the same opinion, "the bullfighter is the cowboy's best friend."

That message, however, doesn't always get from the bull rider to the bullfighter. Bullfighter Dan Newman says, "Sometimes you feel like every bull rider hates your guts."

Buddy and traveling companion Mark Nichols agrees. "The bull riders are pretty focused on what they are doing. I've seen situations where a cowboy has been thrown and he doesn't know where his asshole is and the bullfighter or the clown gets between him and the bull and they get him to safety. And the cowboy just walks away without acknowledging his debt. Sometimes you have to go over to him and say, 'You'd better thank that guy, he just saved your butt.'"

And perhaps his life. If this is the most dangerous sport in North America for bull riders, it is equally dangerous for the bullfighters. Daren Tuftin of Merit, B.C., who's been in the sport for over 12 years, says, "I usually break something every year. I've broken my leg, both my ankles and my shoulder. Ribs – somewhere in the 30s."

"I didn't know we had that many."

"I break the same ones over and over. I've broken everything from my nose to my toes."

Mark had a bull fall on him. "It was New Year's of 1994-95. The bull fell on me and broke my back. And I've had normal bumps and bruises."

I have to bring him back to the topic of his broken back, which he passes over lightly. "I fractured two vertebrae in my back, L5 and L6. It was tough coming back from. You spend a lot of time in the hospital wondering what you are doing with your life. Then you wonder if you can get back in there and do it. It is a mental game and if you get it into your head that you can be hooked, then it gets a lot harder to do the job."

Dan has had his share of injuries. "A bull stepped on my chest. I was five days in the trauma unit. I've blown my knee out. It just wore out." He's been thrown, kicked and hooked. "When he hooks you, you just have to go with it," he says. "You just let him hit you because you're not going to stop it. The important thing is to make sure you're in good position when you land."

Like close to a hospital?

Ricky Ticky Wanchuck had his neck broken in the Wild Horse Race in 1980, but he couldn't wait to get back to rodeoing. "What was I going to do? Stay out of it?" he gives me that look that lets me know I'd be crazy to think such a thing. "I was raised with it, my dad was a horse trader."

Even in the barrel the bullfighters and clowns are not completely safe. Doug Groves got a horn in the back by a Mexican fighting bull while in the barrel. And he's been stepped on while curled up in that confined space.

Why? Why? What is it that makes a man get into an enclosed space with an animal that is not only capable of killing them, but is occasionally willing to do so.

"Because there is nothing like it!"

And there are not too many like Ricky Ticky Wanchuck. He's not a big man, but he's got a big heart, a smile on his face – most of the time – and enough energy to jumpstart a combine. I talked to him just after he came out of the arena in Williams Lake, when he was still breathing hard from the exertion and the excitement. For a 45-year-old he still gets his wheels moving, though Ricky works the barrel now. But even in the barrel the bull can give you a rough ride.

In the off-season the Edmonton lad drives a logging truck, but he enjoys the rodeo and working as a clown makes him feel like he's one of the gang, one of the cowboys. The reason he likes feeling like one of the cowboys is that for many years he was a cowboy, going down the road with the best of them. He was a bronc rider and did the Wild Horse Races – "if you want to talk to someone who's crazy you talk to them" – and now he's a bullfighter.

"What makes a good bullfighter?"

"Good bulls make good bullfighters," he plays with the broken feather that had been on his hat.

He loves the sport and would like nothing more than to do it for another 20 years. "I can't see any better way of making a living. The people are great. I can walk down any mall in America and meet someone I know. I have friends all over the world. There is the odd bad apple, but the fans are great. You can sit in the stands by any one of them and talk to them. A drunk in the beer gardens will get rowdy over nothing, but that's about it. It doesn't happen very often. The people are great."

The next day he's back in the arena, and when he comes out, as he passes me he says, "I'm like a Kansas City Fag. I get all dressed up and go where the cowboys are. Then they beat the shit out of me," he limps away like he's been beaten up.

"Come here, I wanna give you something," he says.

"Yeah?" I raise my eyebrows. Talking about fags, then says he wants to give me something.

From a bag in the back of his truck he pulls out a canary yellow frisbee. It has his name printed in black in a circle. **RICKY TICKY WANCHUCK RODEO CLOWNING ALBERTA CANADA**. In the centre of this it says;

BE SMART . . .

BE DRUG FREE . . .

WINNERS

DON'T DO DRUGS

Cowboys will chew tobacco and drink a lot of beer, but drugs are something the majority of them are not into.

Bullfighters Ricky Ticky Wanchuck (left) and Daren Tuftin at the Williams Lake Stampede.

What they do get high on is the action, the jazz, the danger. Like the time Ricky was down in the States and he'd already finished his act, "I'm changing to go home," he tells the story, "I was already in my running shoes and stripped down to my shirt when the bull started roughing up a cowboy. He was working him over real good. This was one mean bull, Boogey Man. He'd already killed somebody. I jumped in and drew the bull off, and probably saved his life." Ricky talks with excitement. This is what it is all about it. Boogey Man took a tear at him, and gave Ricky a rough time before he could get of the arena, but he had done his job. "That cowboy had red welts all over his body where the bull had hit him. He was down in the mud and you could hardly tell him from the mud. I was a hero in town that night. I couldn't buy myself a drink in the bar."

Although some of the bullfighters and clowns do move between rodeos on a given weekend, they tend to have longer runs in one place than the bull riders. Daren Tuftin was the main clown for the Williams Lake Stampede throughout the four days, giving me the opportunity to talk to him and watch him over a period of time.

Like T Texas Terry, he got into bullfighting because he went to a rodeo where they didn't have a bullfighter and saw the dangers this exposed the cowboys to. When he realized you get a paycheque for every performance, unlike the cowboy who might travel 1000 miles to a rodeo, get bucked and not earn a penny, he was hooked. "I quit everything and started doing bullfighting. I get paid from $500 to a $1000, and it pays the bills."

But it is "pretty expensive going down the road" whether you are a cowboy or a clown, or a bullfighter, and the injuries are an ever-present fact of life. So why does he keep doing it?

"The thrill of it all," he says quietly. "It's a fun life. You see your buddies every weekend. You meet everyone, you get to know the cowboys. You are always on the go. There is no time for lolly gagging."

But there is more. "Once you earn the right to be a professional rodeo clown, once you get there, you don't want to quit. It takes so much work just to get into the business that once you are there, you are going to stay as long as you can."

Daren's act is quite diverse. He doesn't trot out the same thing every day, as some guys do, whether they are at the top of the ladder or playing small rodeos. But whatever they're doing, one thing that the clowns have in common is that they like having a big explosion as part of the repertoire. Daren had his bang during his Elvis impersonation, others have an explosion tied in with almost everything thing they do.

Doug Groves also loves the pyrotechnics, and doesn't mind being close to the fireworks. I caught his act at Cereal. He mixes a concoction of drinks and when he drinks it down it is so powerful it blows his hat off.

"He's crazy," Doug's fiancée Karen Lane assures me. "He singed his head yesterday."

"My hat was getting too old," Doug puts in. "It couldn't take it any more." He points inside a garbage can where there is a worn old hat with a hole in it. Doug takes off his new hat and shows the top of his head which has a scarred bare patch in the middle."

"It doesn't bother me when he's in the barrel," Karen says. "But when bombs go off on top of his head it worries me. He's done that twice."

Daren Tuftin isn't just a clown, he has something to say about bullfighting. "The most important thing about being a bullfighter is that you've gotta be able to keep your head when you're in a storm. If the cowboy gets hung up, you've got to think about what you're doing. You've gotta help the cowboy keep his head. If he gets hurt there is no one to blame but yourself. You've got to be able to think under pressure and do the right things. There is no room for errors. You make too many errors and you won't be at the next rodeo. When everything changes and you find yourself in a storm and that cowboy is in danger, you've got to rise to the occasion."

Despite this pressure, despite the injuries, the travel and all that is part of going down the road, Daren says that it is fun. "If you're not having fun," he claims, "it shows. And if you're not having fun you should stay at home."

Just as the bull riders have taken their sport to new heights, so have the bull fighters. Mark Nichols at 24 has already been in the sport for seven years and won the High School National Finals in bull riding.

"We are professional athletes just like everyone else," he states. "The days of the washed up cowboy who wants to be a clown are over." Bullfighters are trained for the job, and they need physical and mental skills to be able to perform one of the hardest jobs in rodeo.

Mark feels there is a lot of satisfaction in being a bullfighter. "Knowing that you are saving guys' lives, or saving them from serious injury, is a big adrenalin rush."

But there is another aspect to being a bullfighter. Cowboys claim it is exciting and there is no thrill like getting on the back of a bull. Bullfighters have a different perspective.

The bullfighter distracts the bull from the falling rider at the Luxton Pro Rodeo.

"The bull riders are in there for about 15 seconds," Mark points out. "They get that rush the one time they ride. We get it on every one of those bulls."

Young bulls are quick and dangerous, but the bullfighters fear the older bulls more. "Bulls are smart," Mark says. "They're every bit as smart as we are. When they get older we can't outsmart them any more because they've seen it all. They don't fall for your tricks like the young bulls do."

There is a lot happening between bull and bullfighter. "It is a mental game. If you get it into your head that he can hook you then you're going to get hooked."

It takes a lot of composure to keep your head in the face of a rampaging bull and not everyone can do it.

Ricky Ticky Wanchuck tells of a competition held in the U.S. Several guys sit down to a card table set up in the middle of the arena. "They set the table up with cigarettes, drinks and a deck of cards. The guys sit down to a game of cards then they let out a bull. The last man to leave the table wins the jackpot, which can range from $500 to a $1000. The chickens just scatter," he says derisively.

"I saw one show where six guys, all wearing tuxedos, sat down at the table. They were smoking cigars, playing cards and they let the bull loose. It charged right up to the table. Nobody moved. The bull came right up and looked at the table. They all just sat there. Not a man moved. They were ex-bullfighters and they all knew that bulls are attracted to motion."

Rodeos have taken the art of bullfighting to one more level, making it an event on its own. Williams Lake holds a competition in which three bullfighters take on a bull, each day of the Stampede.

"It gives us a chance to show off our skills that we use on an everyday basis," Mark Nichols explains. Putting themselves in danger is what it is all about. "The more you expose yourself to the bull the higher you're going to score. You get more points the more vulnerable you make yourself to hooks, but you lose points if you get hooked, and you lose points if you lose control."

Getting the bull to "work the barrel" adds points to your total, but doesn't do much for the guy who's inside, curled up in a ball, hoping the bull doesn't decide to put a horn into it.

The bulls used for this competition are generally the ranker ones and when they get out in the arena they go after anything that moves. Which isn't always the bullfighter. So he has to get the bull's attention. Which means running after him, getting in his face, then getting out of the way when the bull takes the bait.

The bulls get really worked up. They stop, glare at the bullfighter, paw the earth sending up a dirt and dust shower, lower their heads, snort and charge! From outside the arena the bull looks like a powerful, fierce and frightening force.

"When you are down in the arena with them they look even more frightening," Dan Newman assures me.

That's the jazz.

At the end of the bullfighting event on day two, Mark came out of the arena more pissed off than the bulls. I expected him to start pawing the earth and charge the judges. He thought he'd won the event, but the judges didn't agree.

The other bullfighters, both on-lookers and fellow competitors, agreed with Mark. Mark's rage is such a contrast to the outwardly calm acceptance of their fate by the bull riders. If they disagree with the judges, they almost never take their case to them, and you wouldn't know it from their attitude or their words. The fans are their advocates and often they heartily boo a score. The announcers encourage them to vent their feelings. The booing increases in volume then the announcer laughs and says that it still doesn't make any difference, the judges' mark remains the same.

On day three it was to be Mark's friend and travelling partner, Dan Newman, who not only won the bullfighting event, but wowed the crowd in the process. When the bull cornered him against the railing he jumped over the bull.

"I scraped all the skin off my scrotum," he told me later. They were relaxing after the day's event and I found him and Mark lounging in the parking lot next to Dan's van.

"Did you plan to do that?" I asked.

He nods. "I knew I had to do something spectacular if I was going to win. Last year one of the bullfighters jumped up on the bull and walked along his back from head to rear."

The bullfighters lounge in lawn chairs and sip beer as Dan's family adds a domestic touch to the scene. Dude, a friendly but scruffy looking dog with one brown eye and one blue eye goes to all the rodeos with Dan. "When you take your wife and two children on the road with you it becomes a little more expensive," he says.

Stephanie takes care of Sidney and three week old Daisy. She too was in the rodeo, having grown up around it in Bremerton, Washington. "I did everything," she says. "I did goat tying, riding cows, calf roping . . . I was a Queen. Now I'm a mom!"

Though it may be expensive, it seems to be a price they are willing to pay to give their children a unique experience. "She's been everywhere," Stephanie says of their oldest daughter. "She rocked in Dwight Yoakum's rocking chair."

It is not only the work that the bullfighters like about their professions, they enjoy going down the road.

"I love the travel," Dan says. "You get to see the world while you're working and making a living. You're not getting rich, but you're getting by."

"We have a great time," Mark injects. "One time we brought our own whiskey onto the plane. We got busted, but we didn't care. What were they going to do? Kick us off the plane?"

"It's an adventure," Stephanie says. "You are always meeting someone new."

"You make a lot of friends," Mark agrees. "They are the best friends in the world, but you only see them three or four times a year."

"You travel around going to different towns, and you make friends there, then you go off to another place and you meet the same people. It's really cool."

"They become lifelong friends. Anywhere you go you have friends."

Unlike most people in rodeo, Dan did not grow up on a ranch, nor did he get involved with it early in life. "I played football in school," in his hometown of Eatonville, Washington, "but I had a friend who rode in the rodeo and I'd go down to watch him, but it never dawned on me what he was doing. I never really clued in to what it was all about."

But when he did clue in he was hooked, and six years later he is planning on a long career.

Are there any down sides to the life?

"Sometimes Mark has to come and stay with us," Stephanie teases her friend. "That's a real drag."

"She doesn't like to drive," Dan responds. "I tell her, just drive one more hour."

"Then I end up driving for six hours."

"That's how I get her to drive."

"One time I drove all the way from southern Ontario to Vegas."

Staying with friends is one way to keep the costs down, and you are unlikely to be refused a place to crash. And you would never think of turning down someone who shows up at an odd hour with three people you've never met and they need a place to stay.

Going to 30 rodeos a year means spending a lot of time on the road, and a lot of time in the arena doing 80-90 performances.

I ask Dan what it feels like being inside an enclosed space with a rank bull. Does he get nervous?

"I get butterflies," he admits. "When I don't get the butterflies, then I won't go into the arena. You have to remember," he continues, "that we are there for cowboy safety. That is the most important thing that we do. We are there to save lives. When they get in a bad wreck, you've got to save them.

"It is thrilling. You get in there and you get into overdrive and you go hard all the time."

If they don't, it could mean a cowboy's life, and maybe even their own.

Are there any secrets to riding a bull? I don't know. I wished I knew some. Sometimes things work, sometimes they don't. If there are any secrets to riding a bull, I wish they'd tell me.

Glen Keeley
1989 Canadian Bull Riding Champion

You've Got To Have Heart

What makes a good bull rider? I asked this question many times, and seldom did I get a satisfactory answer. I was often told that a good bull rider was one who knew the basics and executed them well. I was also told that a good bull rider was one who stayed on the bull – yes, but how does he stay on? It is a complicated procedure that requires skill and knowledge.

Not only are there "the basics" to bull riding, but there are a number of factors that are going to determine the nature of a bull ride. The cowboy himself. His training, his experience, his physical conditioning, his present state of mind, how long he's been traveling, injuries and pain, and that undefinable something that the cowboys refer to as "heart" or "try" or some similar word that attempts to give definition to something that is so innately human that words cannot give it form. When you ask a bull rider what makes a great bull rider, you're likely to get an answer such as the one that Don Nahrgang of Bridger, Montana, gave, "A guy that's got a lot of try."

So I had to go at this in another way, and get them to talk about what they were thinking when they got on the bull and what techniques they used once the animal started moving.

The cowboys played down their emotions when they were talking to me. They'd say they weren't thinking much when they got on a bull, but whatever it was they were or were not thinking when they started to settle down on a bull that's kicking and snorting and shitting in the chute, squirming and moving its head trying to get at the cowboy, their faces tell another story. This is serious business. They know that greater and lesser men, better and worse bull riders than themselves, have been killed or seriously injured in less time that it takes to run a 100 yard dash. Though they may keep these thoughts out of the forefront of their mind, the rest of their mind knows the reality. That's the jazz.

In the chute the bull can do them as much damage as when he's out in the arena. The rider, the chute boss and the cowboys helping get everything ready are deadly serious. The rider is focussed as he wraps that rosened rope around his hand, binding himself to an adversary that's much bigger and much stronger. He is only thinking about what he has got to do, and not the fact that the next eight seconds could change the entire course of his life. A 90 point ride could lift him to stardom, money, wealth and women, but more importantly, the chance to ride again tomorrow. He knows that a bad ride, being dumped in the outhouse, could be a worse experience than being dumped in a real shit hole. Death, injury and no money can be the results of a bad ride. All three are top reasons cowboys are forced out of the sport.

The cowboys helping out in the chutes are talking to the rider in low, serious, assuring tones. They call him "cowboy" and that is important to the rider. Being a "cowboy" is something that is earned, and not everyone who wants to be can be.

When they settle down on the bull, the smell in their nostrils, the power between their legs, the crowd waiting and watching, the voices in their ears, their fear being pushed away, they keep their eyes down, head down, their face tightens as the moment approaches. They nod their head and grit or bare their teeth and they go. Preparation is important to the cowboys and that begins a long time before they get to the rodeo.

The five Johansen brothers are Canadian bull riding legends. They all qualified for the Canadian championship, four of them won and Dale took

it twice in '83 and '84. When I met Jack Johansen after the bull-o-rama in Strathmore, my first thought was to ask what made them so good.

The short answer is that they got on 100 bulls every winter. The more you practice, the better you understand what to do. The longer answer is more complex.

Keeping in shape is of utmost importance. "Travel wears you down and if you're not in shape you get 40 miles from home and two days on the road and you're toast."

Bike riding is one of the recommended ways for keeping in shape, as is weight lifting for upper body strength. "You don't want to use heavy weights. You use multiple weights because you've got to keep flexible. You don't want hard muscles. You've got to stretch and keep loose.

"Your reflexes are very important. You've got to keep in top shape. Cowboys can stay in the sport longer as sports medicine gets better and the training gets better."

You've got to stay in the zone, the area between the back where the power is, and the front of the bull, in that area that moves the least. You get too far to the outside and you've lost it.

What attributes does a cowboy need?

"Balance, strength and agility. You're going to have to learn how to roll because you're going to spend time in the dirt."

The mental aspects of it, of course are important. What should a cowboy be thinking during the ride?

"What you should be thinking about is staying on," Jack explains. "You've got to stay straight up and down and you've got to stay in control. You use his (the bull's) momentum to help you and don't get out of shape. As long as you can stay in control then you can stay onboard. There are certain planes you don't want to break."

The other advantage the Johansens had was sibling rivalry. "With five of us to feed off each other, it kept us sharp. There was healthy competition between each other."

Jack was different from most cowboys, who like to prepare themselves mentally a long time before they get on the bull. He was totally different, "I drove everyone nuts because I got psyched up real quick. I stayed loose all the time, right up to the moment that I'd go into the chute, then I was down to business. Other guys would take an hour to get ready."

Glen Keeley, 1989 Canadian champion, spends his time preparing for the ride by stretching and "keeping my mind clear."

"When it works it seems pretty easy," he says. "When it's not working it seems pretty damn hard. Secrets? I don't know. I wished I knew some. Sometimes things work and the next time they won't. If there are any secrets, I wish they'd tell me."

A lot is going on in the cowboy before the ride and they have to try to keep focused and not get too worked up.

Jordie Nash of Blackie, Alberta, though just twelve years old and a steer rider, has already learned the technique of preparing for the ride that will help him throughout his career. "I just think how I'm going to do it. How I'm going to ride it. I stretch and I sit down away from everybody and think about what I'm going to do."

Shane Mills agrees that stretching is important to most cowboys. "I stretch lots before I ride. I like to think about the ride before I go. I like to think about how I can improve it."

Cowboy after cowboy will tell you that riding is a mental game. Clint Ostrem put it this way, "To be a good rider you need focus and determination. And an attention span that is longer than the ride."

"You really have to concentrate," agrees Rick Henderson. "You've got to keep positive thoughts and keep at the basics. Don't get thinking about a bad ride. Everyday's a new game. Anybody can get a 95 on any given day if you get the right draw and if it goes you're way."

You'll get no argument from Gerald James that a great deal of a bull ride takes place in the head. "The good bull riders are better at the mental part of it," he says. "It is not a real strength sport, it takes a lot of balance and technique."

According to Lonny Corbet, one of the reasons that Don Gay was such a great rider and World Champion year after year was that he was so good at keeping square to the bull. "He never got behind the zone."

You have to know what to be focused on, and in two simple words it's "the basics." Shane Mills outlines where you've got to start, "You've got to do the basics. Stay in the middle of the bull, keep your chin down and chest out, and hang on."

Not everyone can say what it is they do on the bull, but they know what not to do. "Don't reach forward," Daryl says, "and don't sit on your pockets. You can't hold on too tight, the bulls are too strong and you don't have the strength to counter him. You have to keep loose. Some bulls buck harder than others and you should know that before you get on."

Kelly McEwan explains a little bit more about why a rider shouldn't sit on his pockets. "Everybody rides similar," he explains, "but you've got your differences. You have to ride the front end and stay away from all the power at the back end. You try to go with the bull. They're too strong to fight or counter them, you have to react to what they're doing."

"You have to have the right movements," Rick Henderson says. "The grip is not as important as you'd think. What is important is to get the feeling of something moving underneath you. Whether it is a horse, a steer or a bull, you've got to learn to move with him."

According to Gerald James the basics means, "Lifting up on your rope, keeping your chin tucked in and your chest out. You have to move your butt around with him. After you've been on enough it's all just reaction. If the bull's coming to the right, if you come back too far with your free hand you can throw yourself off."

That free hand is there for balance and throwing it back helps the rider from going over the bull's head. And should keep him in the zone. Occasionally a guy will throw that hand back too far and too hard and throw himself off the bull. This is difficult for the fans to see, but the other cowboys usually know what happened.

During the 1997 Calgary Stampede, Jim Sharpe did an amazing pirouette off his bull, going straight up, turning and almost landing on his feet behind the bull. That was not completely accidental, though he probably didn't intend to do that. Jim threw his free hand back to give himself momentum to get off the bull when his eight seconds were over. The bull then gave the right bucking motion that combined with what Jim was trying to do and shot him straight up in the air.

Landing far away from the bull is what the riders want when the trip is over, before or after the eight seconds. When a bull stops bucking the cowboy doesn't simply step off and walk away. He'll spur him and try to get him moving and the bullfighter will try to rile the bull into action. If the rider did step off, the bull could suddenly turn on him, and being so close the bull would have the advantage.

Dave Leader outlined the 'basics' in the same words Gerald James used and then he added, "And you turn your toes out so you can get your spurs into him. Posting is when you put your weight on the inside of your legs and pull up on your rope. You post and you reach up here," he puts his free hand up over his head. "You don't want to let the bull lift you. Then you post again and lift."

This is the motion that you see bull riders practicing behind the chutes before they ride.

"You've got to keep moving your feet and loosen them up. You can't hold a death grip on them," Dave warns "or they'll throw you."

He goes through the motions showing me how they move. "It's reaction. You need a lot of reaction skills. You've got to get past the psychological hang-ups. It's about being consistent and keeping your confidence. You have to keep on top of your game. Some guys never develop it and you have to if you're going to be good."

And we all know the good ones have got a heart as big as a truck.

"Everything's happening like that," Dave snaps his fingers three times in quick succession. "It's a huge blur. You don't react to what you see, you react to what you feel. You feel it right here," he slaps the inside of his thighs, "with your legs. It is like the hair on a horse's nose. It's feeling with those hairs. The feelings control your mind. Your body is reacting, not to what you are seeing , but what you are feeling. If you react to what you're seeing it's too late. Right Jim?" he looks up at another cowboy who gives his assent.

"Repetition is so important. When you first start you don't remember shit. But with repetition your body knows what it's supposed to do when it feels this or that."

Dealing with the pressure is as important as riding well and Dave says everybody deals with it differently. He likes to keep a positive frame of mind. "If you start thinking negative things it will affect your riding. You've got to stay positive. Even if you are around another sour son-of-a-bitch, even if you're winning, his negative attitude can bring you down to that slimy, dirty, little pit that he's in. You've got to stay out of it. Then there's Greg Slacuer – he's sour, but he rides good."

Leader, a carpenter by trade, feels that keeping in top condition is important to being a good bull rider. "You've gotta stay in shape or you can't rodeo," he states. "You don't try to get big, but you've got to work out and keep your muscles fit so they can deal with the strain. Your muscles, your joints, your tendons, they all take a hell of a pulling and a strain. You've got to keep them flexible, don't let them get hard and stiffen up on you."

Because of the speed at which things happen, even an experienced bull rider will sometimes not know what happened on his ride.

"Sometimes you'll get thrown off and you won't know why," Gerald James says. "The other guys will be able to tell you."

Though some guys like to study the bulls, watch them as often as possible, both live and on video, and talk to other riders about the bulls, there are some cowboys, like Daryl Palmantier, who have a different approach. "Myself, I don't like to know what the bull does. You make a big plan and it doesn't work out. You just get on and ride. When you're riding you don't really think too much. It's all reaction. Once you've done it enough times your body knows what to do. Your mind follows along."

Leader agrees. "You can overthink a ride, which is what I did in Cereal. I didn't have left on my mind. I expected him to go right. If I'd been there, I would've rode him."

Danny Booth adds another dimension to what it takes to be a good bull rider: aggression.

"Terry West is an aggressive rider," he explains. "He's real focused. You watch him when he draws a real tough bull. You don't let him (the bull) get to you. If you're going to ride the real rank ones, you've really got to ride them. Not just get on them. You've got to use your feet real well.

"A bull is throwing a lot of weight around so it's real important to stay on your rope. Strength is one factor, but not the most important. A big guy is not going to ride any better than a smaller man. The biggest part of this sport is mental."

Then he gets back to "the basics" and he adds a few more ideas to what the basics are. "The equipment, making sure it is in good condition. And learning the proper way to get on the bull. Learning how to do it right."

He suggests that watching the top riders is a good way to do that. Who does Danny like to watch?

The answer is almost predictable, Lane Frost, Cody Custer and Tuff Hedeman. "Jim Sharp is an excellent guy to watch," Danny says. "He always seems to be in control of his ride. Everybody has an individual style and there are variables which will influence how he rides. His size and build and who taught him to ride. There are certain principles that you have to learn.

"You can't override with your free arm. There are certain planes that you don't want to break. Don't ride on your pockets. You want to ride to the front, but not too far. When the judges are judging a ride they will be looking at whether the cowboy is in control. Is he sitting up, is he using his feet, how aggressive is he? Is he making moves on the bull, you just can't sit there, you've got to make moves on him."

Danny, like most other riders, has own ways to prepare for a ride. Going to rodeos, I noticed that few riders pay any attention to the other events. Danny says he usually doesn't even watch the rides ahead of him. "I want to focus on what I've got to do. You want to watch the bulls, so I'll watch them when my ride is over, but I won't watch before I ride."

Like other bull riders, keeping in shape is important to Danny. "I lift weights, run, do calisthenics. Squeeze hand grips and do general weights."

Fear is part of the technique. "I have a little bit of fear when I ride, but it is not something you think about. If there wasn't any fear you probably should quit. I've never turned a bull out because I was afraid. Some of my best rides have been on bulls I was afraid of and I was thinking there was no way I could do this bull. You have to keep your head about you."

His final word on the technique of bull riding, "There are no secrets or magic methods."

Although everyone knows what they should do, executing is another matter:

"That was a piss poor dismount,"

"You got that right."

"He landed right on his face."

A bad landing is not so bad as getting hung up on the bull. Lonny Corbet explains why that happens. "What happens is that you get thrown forward too far, your hand is thrown forward and you get locked to the bull and have to pull the tail of the rope to release it. When thc bull throws you forward, he throws you to the wrong side and your hand gets pinned. If you are right handed, you want to get off the right side. What the bullfighter is doing is trying to get the bull to spin to the left so you can get off on the right. When you want to get off you swing your shoulder over and look to your right. That's where you're going to land. You want the bull to throw you out the back door."

Going over the head of the bull is the worst thing you can do. From there a lot of things can happen, most of them nasty. The bull is in his best position when you're in the worst.

To be a good bull rider you've got to know the basics, but knowing the basics is not necessarily going to make you good. Keeping your fear under control, having some athletic ability and staying on the bull for eight seconds might do it.

Getting In and Getting Out of the Game

Most bull riders on the circuit get into doing rodeo because it is part of their childhood environment. They grow up on ranches where they are close to the livestock and they get to know the animals well. Their fathers, uncles, older brothers, mother and sisters might be in the rodeo, so it is not only a natural progression for them, it is almost expected that they would get involved in one event or another.

A future bull rider gets his picture taken at the Calgary Stampede.

Getting out of bull riding is a much more complicated procedure. It might seem simple on the surface – you just stop riding. But it is not that easy. The sport, the lifestyle, gets in the blood and cowboys keep at it when all reason tells them they should quit. Even once they quit, they miss it, and they long to go back.

Marriage is one thing that gets a bull rider out of the arena. The life of a young man going down the road is not compatible with marriage. The attractions include the night life, the women who find the bull riders very attractive and exciting and are willing to give them a ride of their own. And there are the friends who become family, closer than family, and the drinking and partying and the good times. Spending endless weeks going down the road does not fit in with most people's idea of how to raise a family and keep a wife happy. Occasionally a family will travel together, but it is expensive and difficult.

A lack of money will also make the cowboy find a better way of making a living. Most of them have another job or profession to fall back on, but they go back to their day jobs reluctantly. The majority of cowboys do not make a good living at what they do. And even those who do make what would be a decent living in any other profession aren't that much further ahead once they've paid all the costs of travelling and the entrance fees. Some young men get a lot of support from their families, which gives them the luxury of going down the road with enough cash in their jeans that their winnings become an added bonus.

Injury is most often the decisive factor that makes the cowboy realize that they are spending more time in hospital than in the arena, and that's not how they want to live their lives. A serious injury doesn't mean the end of a career for the cowboy, unless it is so debilitating that they physically can no longer continue. Often the cowboy will return for one season after he's healed up, to show that he hasn't lost it. That he's still got the nerve. But once he's proven himself, he quietly retires. He sometimes believes he'll make a comeback at a later date.

Though the major injury may be decisive, it is the small injuries, the chronic pains, that finally make the cowboy realize the end has arrived. They get tired of living in constant pain and the constant pain limits their ability to ride well, and they can see their career going no further. When they realize they are not going to make their dream of being the best, the rigging bag goes into storage and the cowboy finds away to adjust to life without the thrill of the ride being part of that life.

Cowboys will linger around the rodeo, helping strip the chutes, getting into the arena, becoming pick-up men, becoming clowns and bullfighters, doing whatever they can to keep in contact with the world they know and love.

I've met three fellows who decided against a career in rodeo because of injury.

Daryl Janz is a well-known and popular broadcaster in Calgary. He might well have had a different career if he hadn't had a misadventure with a heifer at an early age.

"I grew up on a farm in Saskatchewan. My father had a combined cattle and grain operation," he told me. "We were all going to be rodeo heros. My dad broke lots of horses and his younger brothers said he was very good at it. I was going to be a bull rider.

"As you know heifers are much better buckers than steers. Having their manhood removed seems to take the buck out of the steer. When I was about 14 we had a yearling and we taught her to buck. I got on her and she was giving me a pretty good ride, but she got up near a barbed wire fence where she bucked me off. I landed on the fence and rode the barbed wire all the way to the ground. It tore my shirt to shreds and my back with it. I have 8 to 10 long scars on my back and doctors often wonder what kind of operation I had. That ended my bull riding career right there."

Daryl seems to be a natural horseman, as he explained with a story about riding in the foothills of Alberta. The horse got a hornet in the cinch and "she went nuts. I rode her for a while then got off her. The friend I was with said, 'You did that like you knew what you were doing.'"

Being in front of the television camera may have its thrills and dangers, but not quite like those of the bull rider.

I was in a bar in northeast Calgary and fell into conversation with Lorne Cheater. He was dressed western, and I thought he might be a stock contractor. He wasn't, but he had a story very similar to Daryl's. He too was raised on a farm and had a brief trip on the back of a steer. The steer didn't do much bucking, until it got near a wood pile where it decided that it had enough of the would-be cowboy and bucked him off. It was a rough landing on the wood pile and it persuaded young Lorne that his rodeo career was over.

Luxton, B.C., on Vancouver Island, is not the centre of cowboy country, but the rodeo itself has a long and rich history.

The first day of the rodeo I saw a young man dressed in blue jeans and a sharp-looking striped shirt, black cowboy hat, cowboy boots, and his reflecting sun glasses completed the "cowboy" image. But it was all fashion. Look up Drugstore Cowboy in the rancher's dictionary and there's a picture of Andy Belfie from Victoria. He had once ridden a bull and he dined out on the story. At the rodeo he repeated his experience over and over, for anyone who would listen.

He was down in the U.S., he couldn't remember exactly where, so we settled on Arizona. "This is the place you wanna get on a bull," he said. "The hospital is just down the street."

For good reasons he knew this.

He decided that this was the time for him to ride a bull, and the rodeo people were willing to let him live his dream. "They told me that the bull always spins to the right. He had been ridden hundreds of times and he always spins to the right. So I got on him and I'm thinking he is going to spin to the right and he spins to the left. He really messed me up. He broke my nose, broke my wrist and bruised my ribs. That was the end of my bull riding career."

"Why did you ride the bull?"

"Because I wanted to."

"Why?"

"It's the way I am. I've got to try everything once, even if I take a beating. I've got to give it a whirl. I enjoyed it, I did have a good time." The guys that enter the bull riding contests that they hold for fans "usually come from the beer gardens." They want to impress the girls, so they get on a bull and end up impressing the doctors at the local hospital with how much beating a body can take, and still survive.

Had that bull turned right rather than left, and had Daryl and Lorne landed on the ground without suffering injury, they might have gone on to careers as bull riders. But where an injury might end a cowboy's career, in these cases, their injuries stopped a career from ever happening.

Smarter Than His Shirt

"A cowboy has to be smarter than his shirt," is one of those sayings that makes the rounds of the rodeo. Most cowboys have become aware of the importance of projecting a positive image. They know they are role models, and they also want to improve the image of their sport to attract more spectators, and more sponsors. The image of the drunken, roughhousing cowboy is not quite a thing of the past, but efforts are being made to clean up that image.

At Cereal I started to take a picture of Jay Manning, who was sitting on the ground taking the tape off his feet after his ride. He had a cigarette hanging out of his mouth. When he noticed me about to take the picture, he threw away the cigarette.

When I protested he said, "We get shit about that all the time. 'You're supposed to be a professional athlete and there you are with a smoke hanging out of your mouth.'"

Most of the cowboys dress very well. Dave Leader, one of the best dressed cowboys, starches his Wranglers.

Most of the cowboys wear Wrangler Jeans, some under the mistaken impression that they are the original jeans. Not true. Levi Strauss went to the California Gold fields in the 1800s; he didn't find gold in the ground, but in a new kind of pants. He noticed that the pants the miners wore couldn't stand up to the wear and tear they inflicted on them in their search for gold. He got material that had been destined to become tents, from which he fashioned the first pair of Levi's blue jeans.

Wranglers is one of the major sponsors of the rodeo, and the cowboys return the favor by wearing their jeans.

As important as their jeans are their cowboy hats. If the cowboy had to choose between wearing only one piece of apparel, a lot of them would having a hard time deciding between their hat, their jeans and their boots.

I've heard that on some occasions they do only choose their hat or their boots. But that's not first hand knowledge.

Jay Manning paid $480 for a new hat, "You buy a cheap one and it won't last the whole season," he explains.

Don Wise is very protective about his hat "I've had it for 25 years. It's been pounded into the ground so many times, but it still holds it shape." A lot of memories associated with that old hat.

He doesn't have much time for people who tell him what the image of a cowboy should be. "One time the Association tried to tell the cowboys how to dress. 'We don't have to dress like cowboys,' was their response. 'We are cowboys. However we dress is how a cowboy dresses.'"

What's the difference between a horse's tail and a man's necktie?

More Bull

In a sport as dangerous as the rodeo, humor is an important element. The clowns are there not only to entertain the crowd but to keep the mood light. A lot of humor that comes out of the situation is much funnier than the planned gags.

If you go to one rodeo you will hear a joke one time, but going to several rodeos in succession, you hear the same jokes over and over again. Do they all share the same sense of humor? Share the same gag writer, or borrow from each other?

I've borrowed from them all. Following is a collection of stories and quips heard at the rodeo. I don't know if they originated there, I'm sure some didn't, but that's where I heard them. If the clowns complain that I'm stealing their thunder, well, it's about time they got some new material. On the other hand, I have no copyright on these jokes, they're not mine and I expect that a clown or two might use them in their next act.

I was in the hotel and I got on the elevator and the chamber maid got on with me. Suddenly she stops the elevator between floors and tears off all her clothes, then she says to me, "Make me feel like a woman!"

So I took off all my clothes and threw them in a heap in the corner and I said to her, "Fold them."

"That cowboy came awfully close to getting an ivory enema there."

"I've got a mother-in-law bigger than that."

"Look at the coat rack on that one."

"That bull's so mean he's only has a number. He doesn't have a name."

"Look how strong that cowboy is, he just picked that bull up with one hand."

Announcer to Clown: I heard you went out after the rodeo and had a few drinks.

Clown: Yes that's true. I had a pretty good time, but I drank a bit too much.

Announcer: That's not good.

Clown: I thought I had better take a cab home.

Announcer: Good for you. You shouldn't drink and drive.

Clown: The RCMP phoned me up this morning . . .

Announcer: Oh?

Clown: They told me to bring it back.

Announcer: Well, did you behave yourself last night after the rodeo?

Clown: Well, I got into a bit of trouble with the police.

Announcer: Oh, what happened?

Clown: I was driving through town and I came to an intersection with a stop sign. I slowed down and there was nothing coming, so I kept going.

Announcer: Uh huh.

Clown: Well, the RCMP saw me and pulled me over. The Mountie comes up to the car window and he says to me, "Didn't you see that stop sign?" I said to him, "I slowed down." He was a big Mountie and he reached right in through the car window, he pulled me out of the car and started beating me on the head with that big flashlight they carry.

Announcer: Really? That's not good.

Clown: I'll say it wasn't. As he's beating me on the head he says, "Now what would you like me to do? Slow down or stop?"

A man goes to a marriage counsellor and he talks to the counsellor who tells him his wife is unhappy because she's not getting enough attention.

"Well, what should I do?" the man asks.

The counsellor says, "She needs to be kissed at least three times a week."

The man says, "Okay. I'll bring her here Mondays, Wednesdays and Fridays."

I'd heard this joke before Lecile Harris told it at the Calgary Stampede, but a slip of the tongue got a bigger laugh than the punch line.

A lady goes into the washroom and sits down on the commode, where some joker has put super glue on it. She gets stuck to the toliet seat and there is nothing she can do to get it off. So they take her to the emergency room.

The woman is very embarrassed and the doctor tries to reassure her, "Don't worry, I've seen it before," he says, "but this is the first time I've seen one with a crack in it."

He had to wait a minute for the laughter to die down so he could get the line out properly, "It's the first time I've seen one with a frame on it!"

I was coming home and I was stopped by the police. He shone the flashlight in my eyes. "You drinking?" he says.

"You buying?" I ask.

His head is so bald it looks like his shoulders are blowing a bubble.

Clown says to a bald man, "You should put some Preparation H on that. It won't grow you any hair, but it will shrink your head to fit the hair you've got."

You know in my business I have to do a lot of travelling, which my wife doesn't always appreciate. But I work hard and when I come home I want to relax. My wife hasn't had a man around the house for a while and she says to me, "When you were away the back door fell off. I'd like you to fix it."

I said, "Woman, do you see the word 'carpenter' wrote on my forehead?"

I went away to work and when I came back a couple of weeks later my wife said to me, "The toilet won't flush. I want you to fix it"

I said, "Woman, do you see the word 'plumber' wrote on my forehead?"

I went away again and when I came back she was complaining that the car wasn't working and could I fix it?

I said to her, "Woman, do you see the word 'mechanic' wrote on my forehead?"

Once again I went away and when I came back three weeks later the back door was fixed, the toilet was flushing and the car was working. I asked her how she got them all fixed.

"The neighbor came over and fixed them all," she said.

"Well, how did you pay for it?"

"I didn't have to. He said I could pay him by either baking him a chocolate cake or by giving him a kiss."

"Well, what did you do?" I asked.

"Do you see 'Betty Crocker' wrote on my forehead?"

A bucking horse goes rank and the announcer says: "If somebody is looking for a gift suggestion for their mother-in-law, this horse may just be the thing."

Clown: I need a policeman.

Announcer: Why?

Clown: Two women are fighting over me.

Announcer: Well, that doesn't sounds so bad, what do you need a policeman for?

Clown: The ugly one's winning.

Clown: I was getting on a bus this morning to come to the Stampede.

Announcer: Yes, what happened?

Clown: There was a woman getting on in front of me and she had on one of those tight short mini skirts.

Announcer: I see.

Clown: Her skirt was so tight that she couldn't step up on the bus, so she reached around and unzipped it a little bit.

Announcer: Did that help?

Clown: No. She still couldn't get on, so she reached around and unzipped it again, but she still couldn't get her leg up high enough. So she reached around once again and unzipped it. Now everyone is waiting and getting a little impatient . . .

Announcer: I bet they were.

Clown: So I helped her on the bus. (He demonstrates with his open palms against the lower part of her anatomy.) She turned around and said, "Excuse me sir, but I don't know you well enough for you to be putting your hands on me like that."

Clown: I said, "Well I think I do. You've just unzipped me three times."

Clown: I had to go to court this week.

Announcer: Misbehaving yourself again.

Clown: The judge said to me, "Do you promise to tell the truth?" I said, "Yes, I do. Judge, you're an ugly man."

Clown: I was going home last night and I flagged down a taxi.

Announcer: Uh hu (being the straight man can be demanding).

Clown: I opened the back door of the taxi and I said to him, "Have you got room in there for a pizza and a six pack of beer?" He said, "Yeah."

"Auuhhhhhhhhh!!!!" he barfs.

Sven and his wife are on holidays in Canada. They go to the rodeo and there's a contest for the audience to see who can ride a bucking horse the longest. Sven goes out and has a great ride and wins the contest. When he goes back to his wife, she says, "Sven, I didn't know you could ride a bucking horse so well."

Sven replies, "Well, remember the winter you had the whooping cough . . ."

Announcer about clown: He should work for the parole board, he never lets anyone finish their sentence.

Announcer: The cowboys like to dress alike and they even use the same deodorant – they all smell like Absorbine Jr.

Why do women have a brain the size of a pea in the morning?

I don't know.

Because it swells in size during the night.

What's the difference between a horse's tail and a man's necktie?

The horse's tail covers the entire asshole.

Glossary

BULLS

Bad Bull – A dirty, no-good, son of a gun. But a bad bull can be a real good bull also. Depends on tone of voice.

Buckers – If he's really good, the cowboy will say, "He bucked through his ass."

Bull-o-Rama – Rodeo event where only bull riders participate.

Drag their Butt – Spins, but just drags his butt around with no real kick.

Eliminator – a bull that doesn't have a pattern/set trip. He's hard to ride. He's not ridden very often.

Flat Spinner – a bull that turns without jumping

Good Spinner – a bull that jumps and turns right back to the gate, and better if they kick up at the back.

Head butt – the bull head butts the cowboy. Sometimes when he's on the ground, and sometimes when he's still on the bull. The bull will jerk the rider down and hits him with his head. "Sometimes you stay on, and sometimes you go to sleep."

Hookie Bull – one that knocks the rider down and tries to hook him.

Hop Skip – the bull sets you up and jerks you down.

Horn Press – Bull gets the rider down and puts his horns to him.

Out of Line – a real tough bull to ride. He'll buck and kick. But if the tone is changed, it can also mean a bull that isn't good.

Rank – an outstanding bull, a bull with a lot of spirit. A real goer. But it can also be used derisively too.

Trip – the movements the bull makes when he's being ridden.

Twister – A good bucking bull who turns a lot.

CHUTE TALK

Chute – the cage where the bull is kept as the rider gets on him.

Chute Boss – Man in charge of the chutes, making sure bulls and riders are ready to go.

Get Her Hot Boys – The chute boss says this to the cowboy when it is his turn to ride.

Heat the Rosen – the wrap rope is rosened to make it sticky. In cold weather they will put on saddle soap first to make it more gooey.

ROPE TALK

Bottom – there are two guys working the ropes, one at the bottom of the bull. "Give me some bottom" – tighten the bottom rope. "You wanna give me some pull?" – tighten the rope. "Pull it up" – Tightens the rope. "Give me a Pinch" – hold the rope in place while it comes around on the second wrap, the spotter holds the rope tight while the rider regrips on the second wrap.

Corner – When the bull makes a quick turn.

Dismounting – The art, or lack thereof, of getting off the bull.

Dropped in the well – the bull spins around in a circle with the cowboy on the inside and he's dropped "in the well."

Fart Knocking – the rider takes a real good beating by the bull.

Flank – a rope which goes around the flank of the bull, which makes him kick out and not crow hop.

Lawn Darted – thrown from the bull and landing on your head.

Sling Shot – when the rider is really thrown from the bull.

Snake Stomping – the rider takes a real good beating by the bull.

Stomped my guts out – the rider takes a real good beating by the bull.

Stripping the Chute – Taking the flank rope off the bull after the ride.

Suicide Wrap – the rope is usually just wrapped around and the cowboy grips it normally. A suicide wrap goes through the fingers. Gives a better grip, but makes it more difficult to get out.

Take Your Wrap – the cowboy is in the chute and they wrap the rope around the bull and around the rider's hand.

Tail – the end of the rope.

GIRLS

The cowboys use most of the common slang for women/ladies/girls: chicks, dream boats, pigs, but they have a few terms of their own.

Auger Hog – very uncomplimentary

Bad Headed – not complimentary

Cut Someone's Grass – A guy in a bar is trying to pick up a girl. When he goes to the toilet or to get drinks, the other guy moves in on the girl.

Easy women:
she's got hinges on her heels
she's got a mattress on her back

Garheaded Girls – not complimentary

Horse Headed – "Girl's got a head on her like a horse."

Hotties – What girls who hang around the rodeo call good looking guys.

Letter "D" Girl – A girl standing against a wall looks like the letter D.

Monkey Wrench Eyes – Girls that give you the look and your nuts tighten up.

Wool – Used as "I've got to get me some wool." Expressing a desire to have sex.

RIDERS

Bad Riders – Riding like Don Knotts (when you're riding very badly.)
Riding like Ned Gump (when you're riding like a nobody.)

Good Riders – He's kicking butt
He's taking the money
He's riding like a wolf
He's the Hot Man

Pea Heart – A guy that talks big in the bar, but his heart shrivels up to the size of a pea when he gets on a bull.

Puss – a rider who doesn't try hard enough. "Don't be a puss."

Riding Slack – Riding in the morning before the main rodeo program. This is done when there are more riders than they can accommodate at the main show.

TRAVELLING

Professional bull riders do a great deal of traveling. They are often paired up with other riders to cut down on costs.

Donut – the steering wheel of a car. "Get behind the donut and drive."

Driving Ivan – A guy who'll drive long distances. "He'll put some miles on."

Going down the road – travelling.

Long Ass Drive – A drive such as the one from Williams Lake, B.C., to Meadow Lake, Saskatchewan, which has to be done from the time the riders finish the event in one location and have to be in the other by the following day when they ride again.

Nondriving pieces of shit – A guy who'll only drive for an hour or so, then want to sleep in the back.

OTHER PEOPLE

Gristle Heads – Calf Ropers and Bull Doggers

Pickup Men – The cowboys in the arena on horses. They will pick the cowboy up after he's been bucked. They round up the stock and get it back into the pens.

Stock Contractor – A rancher who provides bulls, horses, steers and calves to the rodeo.

Townies – People from the local town that are not involved in the rodeo.

VARIOUS

Go Western – When a situation gets out of control, fighting starts. When somebody gets out of control.

Mashing – Digging your knees into the bull to give you a better grip and to agitate the bull. Also, what the bull does to the cowboy when they're in the chute. The bull will mash the cowboy's legs into the rails.

Posting – When riding the bull the rider puts weight on the inside of his legs and pulls up on the rope.

Raspberry – scrapes and bruises

Go Round/Short Go Round – One day's riding/not many cowboys riding that go round.

Printed and bound
in Boucherville, Quebec, Canada by
MARC VEILLEUX IMPRIMEUR INC.
in July, 1999